The Ultimate Solo Lawyer's Guide to More Referrals and Better Clients

A Proven Method to Growing Your Practice

The Ultimate Solo Lawyer's Guide to More Referrals and Better Clients
A Proven Method to Growing Your Practice

Spotlight Branding

First Printing: 2020

Spotlight Branding
9624 Bailey Road, Suite 270
Cornelius, NC 28031

www.spotlightbranding.com

Dedication

To you, the solo/small firm attorney who has spent more time and money than you'd like to admit on marketing that hasn't produced the results you wanted. This book is for you.

Contents

Introduction

Dear Lawyer,

No offense, but most people don't trust you. You're mentioned in the same breath as contractors and tax collectors when it comes to the kinds of people no one wants to work with.

Plenty of surveys over the years have reinforced this idea. For example, an American Bar Association study found that 69% of consumers believe that *"Lawyers are more interested in making money than in serving their clients."*

We both know that's not true. In fact, the vast majority of lawyers we've worked with are dedicated to solving problems and making their clients' lives better.

But that's not how the general public perceives the legal profession. Most of your potential clients are predisposed NOT to trust you.

On the bright side, there is plenty you can do to overcome this perception. And once you do, you're at a competitive advantage compared to all of the other lawyers in your market who haven't figured it out.

The challenge is to establish a personal connection with potential clients so that they can get to know you, sense your passion, and recognize your expertise and your ability to solve their problems. Otherwise, you're just another lawyer who is out to make a quick buck.

There could be many reasons as to why you're reading this book. Maybe you feel distrusted. Maybe you're sick of having the wrong clients show up at your door. Maybe you're tired of the lackluster results of your current internet marketing.

Whatever your reason, this book is here to help you not only break that distrust people have toward you, but it will also show you how to build a marketing ecosystem that maximizes your referrals and positions you as the ultimate expert in your market - and it's all without SEO.

Many lawyers seem to think that internet marketing = SEO. To them, all that matters in the realm of internet marketing is where their website shows up on search results. In fairness, it's hard to blame them – for years now SEO companies have shouted, spammed, and sweet-talked their way into over-priced contracts "guaranteed" to produce results.

If you personally haven't had a bad experience with an SEO company, you likely know someone who has.

Of course there is a place for legitimate SEO work to be done for you. It is important that your website is search-engine friendly and that it shows up when people are searching for help in your practice areas.

But thinking about SEO before you have a solid internet foundation in place is like a retail business spending a fortune putting up billboards and advertisements while their actual store is in ruins and unprepared to serve customers. It's backwards. It doesn't make any sense. That's why you start with referrals.

You're Missing Business That Should Be Yours!

Referrals are an important source of business for most professionals. Every business owner has a referral network of some size – even if it's just a handful of family and friends who send you business once in a blue moon. For most professionals, that network is actually quite large: current clients, past clients, industry colleagues, colleagues in other industries, community leaders, previous employers – the list goes on.

These potential referral sources are people who know you, know what you do and who you help, and trust that you'll do a good job for the clients they send your way.

But for a referral to actually happen, three things must take place:

1. The referral source must have the desire (and the confidence) to send work your way

2. The referral source must have the opportunity to send work your way

3. The referral source must recognize the opportunity and make the connection ("*Oh! I have the perfect person for you...*")

The first two scenarios are taken care of if you do a good job of networking strategically. But #3 represents a major missed opportunity for most lawyers. There are two primary problems as to why this happens:

Problem 1. Your well-meaning referral source **doesn't recognize opportunities** to send you business. It's your job to explain to them what you do, who you help, and to define what a "good referral" looks like. ("*A good referral for me is someone who...*"). You likely do this early in the relationship, but you can't expect the referral source to remember that rule forever. It's important to regularly remind that person of what you do and in what situations you can help people.

Problem 2. Your well-meaning referral source **doesn't think of you** when the opportunity arises. We're all busy. We meet people all the time. We've got a million things going on. In fact, according to researchers, most of us have at least 50,000 distinct thoughts every single day. So it shouldn't be surprising that a referral source you met months or years ago just doesn't recall your name at a moment's notice.

The good news is that there's a simple solution for both problems. **You need to establish regular touch-points with your referral network**. Those touch-points should serve the simple function of reminding your network that you're still out there, but they should also remind them what you do, who you help, and what a good referral looks like. Most importantly, these touch-points should reinforce your credibility and your expertise as much as possible.

There are a number of ways to create these touch-points. For example:

- Send birthday gifts and holiday cards
- Eat lunch together
- Make phone calls to check in

- Send resources – interesting books, articles, ideas
- Connect on social media and maintain an active presence (This allows you to create multiple touch-points every single week!)
- Send out regular e-newsletters

The list goes on, and the best approach is a combination—multiple touch-points through different platforms so that you maintain top-of-mind awareness. This book will look deeper into everything you can do and why you should do it.

It Might Be Time to Rethink Your Marketing Strategy

When we ask lawyers what they need their marketing to accomplish for them, the most common answer by far is "*I need more clients.*" But we'd like to challenge that mindset. Do you really need more clients… or do you need *better* clients?

Take a moment and think through the clients you've worked with over the past several months. How many of them:

- Didn't pay you on time, in full, or maybe didn't pay at all
- Consumed a ton of time and energy in the engagement/consultation process before hiring you (or worse, not hiring you despite the time you invested)
- Were rude or disrespectful towards you, your time, and/or your team
- Didn't trust you
- Needed help with matters outside of your area of focus
- Drained you rather than energized you

Whether your answer was "*a couple*" or "*almost all of them*," your marketing strategy should be revised to get rid of those people.

Here's an analogy for you.

On one end of the spectrum you have Wal-Mart—cheap, always open, stores all over the country, and you can get almost anything there—although the quality may be questionable.

On the other end of the spectrum, you have high-end retailers like Neiman Marcus. Expensive, restricted availability, and a very narrow selection of extremely high quality merchandise.

Wal-Mart makes money through *volume*. They have tiny profit margins, but they're so efficient and they sell at such high volume that, as a company, they're very profitable. Neiman Marcus and other high-end retailers make their money through higher margins. They sell to a much, much smaller number of customers than Wal-Mart, but they've built a brand that allows them to create much higher margins than Wal-Mart. They don't need a high volume of customers. They need the *right* customers.

For them, it's not about quantity, it's about **quality**.

Now, which end of the spectrum would you like your law practice to operate in? Would you rather be a (relatively) low-cost provider of a wide variety of legal services, making your money through high volume? Or would you prefer to build a focused, lower-volume, higher-margin practice?

We can't answer that question for you. But we can tell you, generally speaking, that focusing on a niche, building a brand, and working with a smaller number of carefully selected clients will result in:

- Less time working
- Ability to charge higher rates
- More referrals
- More repeat business
- More fulfillment with your work

Keep that in mind as you read through this book. Figure out what you want your practice to look like. Is it quantity and high volume? Or is it quality and a more focused practice?

Once you've identified your direction, your marketing can help you get there, and that's where this book can really help you out.

Action Item: Set Your Goals

Grab a piece of paper and write down what your firm would ideally look like. How many cases do you want to take on each month? What would your annual revenue be? What kind of cases would you prefer to take?

When you have those ideas written down, you can take your annual revenue number and divide that by how many cases you'd take on each month (multiplied by 12) to generate what you would need your average case value to be. Compare that number to where you are right now.

Whether you're already close to that number or so far off that you're considering a career change, keep that piece of paper handy and refer back to it as you implement the strategies in this book. You won't see changes happen overnight (no good marketing plan works that fast). However, you can look back on this in a few months and a couple of years to see the progress you've made.

Chapter 1 ~ It's All About Referrals

This is a hard truth to accept, but your referral framework is broken! If it wasn't, you probably wouldn't be reading this book.

The problem is that it's hard to tell that it's broken. After all, you (like many attorneys) are probably getting a decent amount of referrals already. Even in today's digital marketing world, a lot of business still comes from word of mouth, whether that's from past clients, other attorneys, or strategic relationships in specific industries.

However, no matter how many referrals you are currently getting, the data says that you are missing out on so many more! According to a study produced by Texas Tech University School of Business, 83% of your clients are willing to refer to you. But, **only 29% actually are**. In other words, you are only getting about one-third of the referrals that you should be getting!

This is a big issue that often gets overlooked. With more and more marketing companies reaching out to you every day, selling you advertising, pay-per-click, or promises of a high Google ranking, it is easy to lose sight of all the referrals you are missing out on. How much revenue are you losing simply because you're not tapping into that other two-thirds of referrals?

Furthermore, referrals are often better clients than those who find you online. This only compounds the issue. Not only are most law firms receiving fewer referrals than they should be, but when they do spend time, money, and other resources on their marketing, it is often focused on attracting more clients from advertising than it is focused on generating referrals.

Did you know that it costs up to 25 times more to generate new customers versus marketing to your existing contacts? That statistic alone should cause you to put this book down and go cancel your agreement with your SEO provider.

The good news is that it's not complicated to fix your broken referral framework. The biggest culprit in this issue is a lack of staying top-of-mind. The days of an annual holiday or birthday card to your clients being enough have passed. We all have too much going through our lives every day to keep up with. It is simply too easy to forget about you and what you do.

When the moment arises to make a referral, people just don't think of it. They don't make the connection to you, whether it's because they forgot about you or (more frighteningly) another attorney did a better job of staying top-of-mind than you. However, the more you stay connected with your network, and the more you remind them what you do, the more likely they are to think of you first in the moment it matters.

Marketing strategies such as an email newsletter, a consistent social media presence, and blog content that focuses on people, not search engine robots, can go a long way in keeping you well connected with your network and ultimately fixing your broken referral system. You just have to be smart about it, and fixing this broken framework is one of the best decisions you will make for your law firm! This book is designed to show you how to do just that.

It all starts by focusing on your existing assets and resources. What do you already have in place that you can do a better job of leveraging? For most lawyers, the first item on that list is their network – their relationships. Your network of current clients, past clients, colleagues, supportive family and friends, and others is a valuable asset that holds the potential for significant growth. But when you talk to most marketing companies—especially internet marketers—you won't hear a word about leveraging relationships. Instead, the focus is on cold lead generation—often through SEO or pay-per-click advertising.

Certainly there is a time and place for that type of advertising, but it doesn't make sense to spend thousands of dollars on a new, speculative campaign when you have existing resources at your disposal that aren't being leveraged to the fullest. Whether you're just starting your own firm or you've been in business for decades—you should not be spending a single cent on cold lead generation until you've built a system to maximize your referrals.

Why? Because referred clients are generally superior to new clients from other sources for a handful of significant reasons. That's why it makes sense to focus your marketing on referrals first. Here are five reasons why this is the case:

1: It Reduces Your Cost of Acquisition

Referrals are far less expensive to generate than any other type of client. There's often no direct cost, and even when you factor in referral-generating tools such as an email newsletter and social media marketing, the cost-per-client for referrals is typically much less than a client-generated through other forms of advertising.

It's logical when you think it through – it takes much less momentum to leverage an existing relationship than it does to create new leads out of thin air. If you've never run the numbers for your firm, take some time now to do so. We can practically guarantee that your cost of acquisition for referrals will be significantly lower than your other lead sources. A lower CoA means higher margins for your practice and more take-home pay for you!

2: It Builds Instant Trust

One of the hardest tasks for every business is persuading the client or customer to take the leap of faith—to pull out their wallet, sign on the dotted line, and move forward. It's particularly difficult in the legal field because the stakes are higher and the dollar amounts are significant (not to mention that whole "people don't trust you" thing we noted at the beginning).

Building your practice through referrals helps you circumvent this—because when a trusted friend or colleague makes a referral to you, their trust and credibility is transferred to you. You don't have to start from scratch because someone has already vouched for you. This shows up in the form of higher conversion rates.

3: It Avoids "Sticker Shock"

There's nothing more frustrating than having a great conversation with a prospective client, feeling like you're aligned and that there's a great opportunity, only to have them freak out when they find out how much your services are going to cost. Referred clients generally know what to expect with regard to your rates, and they typically won't reach out to you if they can't afford you.

Today's crowded legal marketplace makes this an even more significant issue—there are more than 1.3 million lawyers in the United States and you have plenty of them in your market. But that's only the tip of the iceberg when it comes to the competition you're facing. Websites like LegalZoom provide document creation services for dirt-cheap prices. For example, pricing for a Last Will and Testament starts at $89. As a result, many prospective clients have unrealistically low expectations when it comes to price. You shouldn't be a "bargain basement" firm, and clients that come to you through a referral will know this ahead of time.

4: It Creates Mutual Respect

We've all dealt with nightmare clients—those who abuse our time and abuse our staff, or who simply have unrealistic expectations and become frustrated when the engagement doesn't play out the way they expected it to. A client who is referred to you is less likely to go in this direction. There's a preexisting relationship because of the mutual relationship you have with the individual who made the referral.

If you look back at it, you'll likely find that, most of the time, referred clients are easier to work with than clients who came to you through other sources. Don't underestimate how big of a deal it is to work with clients that you and your staff genuinely enjoy working with. In particular, we've seen a big difference in clients who come through referral as compared to clients who find you via Google search. Google traffic tends to be much more transactionally-focused. You'll experience this most directly with regards to your pricing, but it often bleeds into the relationship as a whole.

5: They Are More Likely to Refer to You in the Future

Clients who have been referred to you are statistically more likely to make referrals in the future, creating the possibility for an endless chain of referrals. There have been a variety of studies on this topic, but the best breakdown we've seen comes from a book entitled the *No*

B.S. Guide to Maximum Referrals and Customer Retention by Dan Kennedy and Shaun Buck. Go read it when you're done with this book.

Do you see where we're going with this?

Referrals are easier and less expensive to generate than cold leads. They tend to convert at a much higher rate. They're less price sensitive, more pleasant to work with, and more likely to make referrals of their own in the future. Referrals truly are the low-hanging fruit when it comes to growing your law firm. Focus on maximizing your referrals before you spend money on speculative marketing and advertising to the outside world.

At the end of the day, make sure you have the mechanisms in place that make a big difference. Social media, video, and your email newsletter are powerful tools for referral generation (and we'll get to this later on). But there's no substitute for getting out in your community, creating relationships, and demonstrating your credibility. Two of the best ways to do this are:

1. Pursuing speaking opportunities that get you in front of potential clients and referral sources

2. Hosting networking events of your own—even something as simple as a monthly lunch-n-learn or networking breakfast

Both of these strategies work well to raise your profile, increase visibility, and position you as the obvious choice for referrals. And of course, make sure that you capture contact information at every opportunity so that they can be plugged into your follow up system. That's how you keep them engaged and get them to think of you first whenever the opportunity arises!

<u>Action Item:</u> Collect Past Data

Go through your past sales data (you have sales data, don't you?) and compare the following:

• How much money you spent marketing to someone who was a referral versus someone who came in through other marketing efforts. (This is otherwise known as the Cost of Acquisition or CoA.)
• The conversion rate between your referrals and other leads

You should see a dramatic difference between your referred clients and those you found with cold lead generation. If you don't have any of this data, start tracking it now! How else are you supposed to be able to measure the effectiveness of your marketing?

Chapter 2 ~ Getting Started

You can't truly dive into a marketing strategy without understanding what goes into it. It all starts with understanding your target market. This is true for businesses of every size, and it's true for your law firm.

In order to effectively market yourself and your services, there are a number of fundamental questions you need to be able to answer regarding your target market. Without this information, you're flying blind. You're sitting at the controls of an airplane with no idea how to reach your destination, hoping that you'll get lucky and see it appear on the ground beneath you. (It almost certainly will not.)

Before we get into the details, note that there is a difference between knowing how your target market thinks, and knowing how *you* *think* your target market thinks. You may assume that you have the answers, but that assumption could cost you huge amounts of money.

Don't assume. Spend enough time immersed in your target market that you **know** how they think. Read their industry publications. Attend their trade meetings. Spend time with individuals and ask them questions. Test various messages and communication channels until you know what works.

Here are four specific questions that you should be able to answer:

1: Who are your ideal clients are and where you can find them?

If you ask most lawyers who their ideal client is, they'll tell you that it's "*anyone who can afford my retainer.*" That mindset leads lawyers to chase any client with money—whether or not the lawyer enjoys performing the type of work that needs to be done, whether or not the client is a jerk and a complete pain in the butt to work with, and whether or not the lawyer is particularly skilled in that specific area of law.

Don't be afraid to identify a niche and narrow your practice. Once you've done that, find out where your ideal clients gather. Figure out which networking functions they attend, which LinkedIn groups they belong to, which websites they visit, which radio stations they listen to, which conferences they attend, and so on. Build a presence in those places.

2: What keeps your ideal clients up at night in fear?

What are your clients afraid of? What stresses them out? Are they afraid that they are going to lose their house in foreclosure? That they are going to lose a lawsuit and lose everything dear to them? Lose their kids in their divorce? Lose their good reputation and perhaps even lose their freedom?

When you legitimately understand their fears, you can address those fears with your marketing, and that's powerful. If you position yourself as knowledgeable, empathetic, and uniquely qualified to prevent their worst fears from becoming a reality, you're in a very good place.

3: What do your ideal clients *really* want to get out of their relationship with you?

Similarly, identify the often-unspoken *upside* that clients are hoping you will be able to provide. A business owner isn't looking for a good business lawyer just so that he can get transactional work done, he wants a good lawyer so that he can sleep well at night. He wants to enjoy time on the golf course. He wants to know that his lifetime of work is in good hands and that his kids will be able to enjoy the fruits of his labor.

Don't focus on the nuts and bolts that your clients need to purchase. Take the time to understand **WHY** they want to purchase them and you will be able to communicate on a much deeper and more inspiring level.

4: How do you speak their language?

How does your target market communicate? Chances are they don't speak and write in the same way that you learned to speak and write in law school, or in the same way you speak and write to your fellow lawyers. Don't use technical and legal jargon that doesn't make sense to your audience. Learning how to speak and write the same way your target market does allows you to communicate in a way that makes sense to them. It inspires trust and it gives them a compelling reason to hire you instead of some other lawyer who just doesn't get it.

What does this have to do with your marketing? Everything.

Your website, your social media profiles, your video, your e-newsletters, and so on are marketing tools first and foremost. Everything about them—from their design to their content to their function to their delivery—needs to be calibrated and built for maximum appeal to your target market. And until you know who your clients are, where you can find them, what they're worried about, what they're dreaming about, and how to communicate in a language that resonates with them, you can't create an effective internet marketing presence.

It Starts with the Right Mindset

Before you start any marketing initiative, you need to have the right mindset. We've attended several bar conferences and other conventions and met thousands of lawyers. However, we continue to meet lawyers who are afraid of growth. They may not have even been conscious of that fear; rather, their own mindsets trapped them into making decisions that would ruin their chances of success.

When lawyers stop by our booth at events, almost every conversation follows the same script. After we ask what their specialty is and explain we do marketing for law firms, they shrink back from investing in our services, giving a variation of the same excuse: *"I'm just a solo."* When we ask what they mean, they say, *"Oh, it's just me and a very small staff. We just don't have all the marketing that big firms have."*

That's a poor man's attitude. While they may have limited resources, solo and small law firms actually need marketing more than the big firms. Big law firms do their marketing in-house because they

15

have staff specifically for that, but small firms can't afford that luxury.

Here's the reality: **If you can't afford to do marketing, you can't afford to have a law practice.** Clients will still trickle in, but, instead of running your firm, you'll just have an awful job. You'll still work 12-15 hours per day just like when you were slaving away at a big firm, but instead of enjoying the perks that firm offered like in-house office administration, marketing, and bookkeeping, you have to do it all yourself on top of all the legal work. If you want to avoid that fate, find a way to invest in marketing.

We have two theories about the source of the *"I'm just a solo"* line. We already mentioned the first one: That lawyers have a subconscious fear of growth. They're afraid their lives might be worse if they grow too much, and they're worried that if they load up with more clients, they'll have less time for their spouse and kids.

They're thinking, *"I'm already stressed now because I'm a solo running my own firm. How much more stressed am I going to be if I get even busier?"* Still, ask any one of them if they want to grow their practices, and they'll probably say yes. Buried underneath that "yes" is that fear, and it's paralyzing them.

What those lawyers don't realize is there's both a right and a wrong way to grow. We know dozens of solo and small firm attorneys running seven figure practices, and, while they have to deal with staff (some associates, an office manager, a paralegal, a secretary, etc.), their lives are far better than they used to be. Those lawyers have more free time because they've hired people to handle the larger, more time consuming aspects of their cases. Managing people is tough, but it's a lot less stressful than struggling to get by every month, wondering where your next retainer will come from. The bottom line is this: Don't be afraid of growth. Invest in marketing, and you'll end up with more time, more money, and more freedom to take that family vacation or do whatever it is that you really want to do.

Our second theory about the *"I'm just a solo"* attitude is that lawyers are feeling the weight of limited resources. *"I'm just a solo,"* they're thinking. *"I don't have the money the big guys do."* We understand that, but you can reverse your situation by investing in the right places (which we'll show you later on in this book). Be smart and savvy about where you spend your money. Do the math on how big of a return you'll get from your investment, and you'll never hesitate to spend on good marketing.

So, next time you catch yourself thinking "*I'm just a solo*," stop and examine your mindset. Are you setting yourself up for failure or success? Don't let fear hold you back.

It's Time to Humanize Your Marketing

Something strange happened to the marketing world when the internet and Google became integral parts of our lives. Marketers quickly abandoned the strategies and principles that had worked for centuries (the first evidence of any sort of branding and marketing appeared as far back as 35 AD in Pompeii) and replaced it with search engine lead generation. Today, far too many lawyers equate internet marketing with showing up on the first page of Google.

However, the same strategies that worked before the internet— i.e., word of mouth, referrals, and branding—still work today, and arguably even more effectively when you use the internet. We're not saying that Google isn't important for professionals, but **internet marketing is much bigger than Google**. However, when firms focus their marketing solely on Google, it rarely works out for them.

Rather than reaching out to the humans that they want to do business with, they end up using marketing strategies that are focused solely on manipulating Google's algorithm. It results in spammy blog posts stuffed with long keywords and website content that no human would actually read. They blast out hundreds of social media posts per week, far more than any human wants to sort through. They purchase email lists and send out unsolicited junk to thousands of people that they've never met. And so on.

These tactics just don't work well. They *might* eventually get you on the first page of Google temporarily, but unless your website and the rest of your internet presence are engaging, inviting, and clearly communicate what you do in human terms, your position on the search engines doesn't really matter.

Think of it like this: You see print ads, billboards, television commercials for a local restaurant. You hear their ads on podcasts and the radio. When you finally go check it out, the workers are unprofessional, the menu doesn't look appealing, the sanitation grade is below a 90. How likely are you to eat there again? Hopefully not likely.

That's the equivalent for attorneys who only focus on SEO and don't put much work into any other marketing. People can find them on the first page of Google, but they'll go to a website that looks awful and doesn't clearly convey how that attorney can help them.

The problem is that many internet marketers aren't actually marketers at all—they are engineers and mathematicians. They know how to manipulate search algorithms, but not how to build a brand and connect with an actual audience. That's why most lawyers have been told to focus on SEO with no thought about what else goes into a successful marketing strategy.

Here are four quick ways to "de-robotize" your marketing and connect more effectively with your audience:

1: Stop artificially stuffing your website content with keywords

It's great to use relevant keywords in your website content when you can and when it's natural—but we've all seen those websites where every other sentence starts with *"An Experienced Florida Divorce Lawyer..."* This type of content is irritating for your website visitors, hard to read through, and makes YOU seem like a robot, not a human with a pulse. Instead, focus on creating website content that shows your prospects that you understand their needs, that you care, and that you are the best solution for their legal needs.

2: Stop over-posting and over-promoting on social media

Social media is an excellent way to connect with your audience, but don't overdo it. Post no more than a couple of times per day at the very most. And even more importantly, make sure that your content provides value to your audience—don't hit them over the head with endless sales pitches. If all you do is promote yourself, your audience will quickly tune out. Give them content that they'll actually want to read or watch.

3: Stop spamming your mailing list

First, avoid sending email to people you don't know and who haven't interacted with your firm in some way. Purchased mailing lists are rarely a good idea. Your mailing list should comprise of people who have dealt with you in some way—as a client, as a referral source, as an attendee at a seminar you participated in, etc.

Second, you have to make your email valuable. Give them a reason to care. Include informative blog entries, news that impacts your industry, thought-provoking ideas and quotes, and so on. Make it worthwhile and valuable!

4: Focus on creating valuable content

The silver lining in all of this is that the best way to actually perform on search engines is to create valuable, quality content—not just a ton of content for the sake of having a ton of content. Google's stated goal, and the goal of every search engine, is to provide the best and most valuable content to people that are searching. People panic every time Google changes its algorithm. But if you look closely, the people who are panicking are generally the mathematicians and engineers who focus on manipulating the rankings rather than just creating excellent, relevant, and valuable content to begin with.

Action Item: Content Audit

Conduct an audit of your website's content. How does it read? Are the headlines and copy stuffed with keywords that make it a clunky and boring read? Have your staff read your website's copy and get their honest feedback. If it's uninspiring or downright awful, look into having it rewritten.

What's Your Unique Selling Proposition?

Most conversations about marketing a law firm—or really, most businesses—are focused on the medium, not the message. It's easy to get distracted by bright shiny objects—*"Should we try AdWords? What about SEO? Or maybe a billboard?"*

Those are good conversations to have. The problem is that most firms aren't first having a conversation about their marketing message. The channels you use to communicate your message are only as good as the message itself.

At the core of your marketing message lies your Unique Selling Proposition (USP.) It should answer the following question:

Why should a customer choose to do business with me instead of another lawyer, a cheaper option, or nothing at all?

It's exceedingly rare that a client will absolutely have to do business with you. The legal market is more crowded than it has ever been. It's almost certain that there are other lawyers in your market who offer the same services as you do at rock-bottom rates. Even more, internet-based services offer forms and other legal services for even less. For example, LegalZoom offers to create a Last Will and Testament for $89, trademark registration for $199, and work visas for $1,495.

The option of doing nothing is a real threat as well. Consumers regularly avoid hiring a lawyer due to cost—even middle and upper-income consumers.

The job of your marketing is to give your clients a compelling reason to take action—to show them why investing in your services is an investment they can't afford NOT to make.

An effective USP creates clear differentiation. Consider these companies and their USPs:

• *World Class Insights That Generate World Class Results.* (Deloitte)

• *When it absolutely, positively has to be there overnight.* (FedEx)

• *Fresh, hot pizza delivered to your door in 30 minutes or less or it's free.* (Domino's Pizza)

Each of these selling propositions differentiated their respective businesses and created billions of dollars in revenue. In each of these examples, there is a very clear and compelling reason for their customers to choose them instead of all other options, including cheaper options and the option of doing nothing.

Developing your USP starts with selecting the right target market. Your ideal clients should have a need for your services AND the ability to pay the rates that you're happy with. It's very difficult for any small business to thrive by competing on price because clawing out a high income on tiny margins requires a transaction volume that's not realistic.

Once you've zeroed in on your target market, answer the following:

• **Who are your ideal clients?** The more detailed your profile, the better. How old are they? What's their average income? What languages do they speak? Where are they located geographically?

• **What are their pain points?** What are their (often unspoken) fears as it relates to your services? For example, entrepreneurs worry that their life's work and everything they've put in the bank could be wiped away by an angry customer or an unfortunate accident. They're not really looking for a business attorney because they have a transactional need—they're looking for someone who can help them sleep well at night, secure in the knowledge that their lifetime of work is protected.

• **What are their goals?** This is the other side of the coin—what are your clients really hoping for beyond their transactional needs? An immigration attorney isn't selling complicated paperwork—he's selling the opportunity to be reunited with loved ones or the opportunity to pursue the American dream.

With this background information in place, look for opportunities to differentiate your practice and add superior value to your services. There are several ways to consider doing this. You can offer:

- Faster service (guaranteed call-back within X hours)
- More personal service (direct access to the owner/partner)
- Services above and beyond the basics
- Flexible payment structure
- Experience (*"Been there, done that, I've seen it all."*)
- Specialized focus (*"I'm not a jack of all trades, I focus exclusively on..."*)
- First-class experience (Your staff, your office, your communications)
- Exclusivity (*"We have the only solution that includes..."*)
- Convenience (Extended hours, convenient location, streamlined process)

There are no one-size-fits-all solutions here—you'll have to put the pieces together. A good unique selling proposition will likely combine one or more of these concepts in a way that creates a unique and compelling value for your target market.

With a rock solid USP in place, you've done the hard work. Now make sure that your value proposition is properly communicated—on your website, on social media, by your team during consultations, and across all of your advertising and business development channels.

NOTE: Your unique selling proposition is *not* the same as a slogan or tagline—although there can be overlap. It may be explicitly stated, but it doesn't have to be. What's important is that your value proposition is clearly conveyed to your target market, using language that resonates with them and positions you as the right solution for their needs.

Action Item: Create Your USP

Using the steps above, create your firm's USP. While the actual USP itself should be no more than a sentence or two, the information you need to fully inform it could be several pages long. After all, you need to:

1. Identify your target market
2. Build a highly detailed ideal client persona (or multiple personas)
3. Identify the pain points you address with your services
4. Identify the goals you help your clients accomplish
5. List all of the benefits/perks your firm offers better than any other attorney in your market

Once you have that information, you can condense it down to your Unique Selling Proposition.

Create More Than Customers—Create Raving Fans!

When it comes to customer service, what is your goal? For many business owners, the answer is *"satisfied customers."* They strive to provide a quality product or service and create a pleasant enough experience to ensure that the customer walks away satisfied and that he or she becomes a repeat customer.

But aiming just to satisfy customers is setting the bar too low. Instead, your goal should be to create raving fans.

Raving fans are customers that aren't just satisfied—they're customers who can't stop singing your praises to everyone who will listen. Raving fans will recommend you to their neighbors, their family, their friends, and anyone else they can find. And because there are few marketing tools more powerful than sincere word-of-mouth recommendations, raving fans are valuable assets.

The slight downside is that it requires an investment of additional resources on the part of a business owner. But when you consider the benefits, both short and long term, it's an easy decision. Here are three practical steps that you can take to create more raving fans of your business:

1: Ask your customers what they want

Customer surveys are a valuable tool—at the very least, make it a goal to send out a survey annually. You can do this via direct mail, email, or online (utilizing free platforms such as SurveyMonkey). Ask them what they like about your business, what they'd like to see changed, and what (if anything) you could do to meet their needs even more effectively.

2: Never say "no"

Clients and customers will often make requests that are outside of the services you offer. Rather than turning them down, refer them to an individual or business that can meet their needs. This simple step will help you build a reputation as a business that always has a solution.

3: Manage expectations

Expectations play a significant role in establishing your customers' perception of your business. Promising results in five days and not delivering until day 10 is a disappointment—while promising results in 15 days and delivering in 10 is exceptional. Managing the expectations you create ensures that you are always in position to impress your customers and clients.

Marketing Your Benefits, Not Your Features

As you market your products or services, what is your message focused on: features, or benefits?

Features are qualities or characteristics that your products and services offer. If you are selling laptops, for instance, features would include the speed of the processor, the size of the hard drive, and the screen resolution.

Benefits, on the other hand, focus on the *results* your customers will get from using your products and services. Benefits of a laptop may include the ability to store priceless family photos and home videos, the ability to run complex programs and games, and providing great viewing experience for videos and games.

Ultimately, customers in your market will choose to buy from you or not based on the benefits that they perceive in your products and services. They don't care about the technical specs of a laptop—they want to know what it will do for them.

Therefore, focusing on features while marketing is risky at best because you're depending on your audience to recognize the features you are advertising and translate them into benefits for themselves. This works in some cases—for instance, savvy computer users know that a one-terabyte hard drive offers ample space to store a large home video library. But plenty of potential customers don't know enough to translate these features into benefits, and as a result, they won't recognize the value of your products and services.

There's an old saying that, when you're selling a shovel, you shouldn't focus on the shovel—you should focus on the hole your customer can dig with it. No matter what type of business you may own, this is important advice.

Take a moment to evaluate your marketing message. Are you focusing on the features and technical specifications of your products and services? Or, are you focusing on the unique benefits that your customers and clients will receive when they choose to do business with you?

<u>Action Item:</u> Identify Your Benefits

Look at the legal services you provide and make a list of the benefits those services create for your clients. Remember, no one cares that you file paperwork or go to court. They care about what happens after the paperwork is filed and the verdict is rendered. For example:

- You provide peace of mind
- You protect assets
- You pave the way to pursue dreams
- You give people a new lease on life
- You secure someone's legacy

Whatever the benefits may be for your practice area, make sure they're clearly conveyed in your marketing message.

Don't Compete on Price!

When it comes to pricing their products and services, many business owners make a simple calculation: if the prices are set as low as possible, without losing money on the deal, we'll maximize our share of the market and our profits. It works for Wal-Mart, right?

Well, yes—but that's because Wal-Mart's massive size allows them to control all of the key variables all the way along their supply chain. And it's because their overwhelming volume of sales enables them to turn small margins into massive profits each year.

Most small businesses don't have either of these advantages. So what happens?

Pricing products and services below market rates is usually successful in the short term, assuming you can get the word out. It's not hard for your firm to build up a solid clientele of bargain shoppers. But here's the problem: As soon as a competitor finds a way to undercut your prices, your customers vanish. Why?

Because the only reason your business brought in customers was due to your low prices. There was no loyalty, other than loyalty to a low price.

What's the solution? What can your firm do if it lacks the massive resources of a Wal-Mart?

Forget competing to offer the lowest price in your market. Instead, **focus on providing value** by positioning your business in such a way that customers and clients are willing to pay a premium for your products and services..

Think about it for a moment—do you buy the cheapest car you can find? Do you take your kids to the cheapest dentist you can find? Do you trust your taxes to the cheapest accountant you can find? Probably not, and here's why: because the service providers you choose offer enough value that you're willing to pay a premium for them.

So forget price. Instead, focus on providing value. Providing value builds loyalty. It offers immunity against competitors who slash prices to win business, and it allows you to make more money.

So how should you make yourself attractive to potential customers?

1: Position Yourself as the Expert

Imagine for a moment that you're looking for a new family dentist or a new accountant to handle the taxes for your business. Who are you going to look for? One of the most crucial factors is almost always expertise. We want the best for our families and for our business—and your customers are no different. Work towards becoming a recognized expert in your industry, and you'll find that customers will begin actively seeking you out. Specifically, consider:

- Starting an industry-centered blog
- Establishing a credible social media presence
- Writing and publishing articles online
- Investing in a website that establishes credibility and expertise
- Speaking to networking groups, seminars, etc

• Publishing a book

2: Differentiate Yourself from Your Competitors

The more unique that you can make yourself and your business, the better off you'll be. When it comes to generic commodities, like gasoline or a gallon of milk, price is often the determining factor. You want the opposite—to be so unique that you are the only choice for your customers. Leverage your unique assets—your experience, your knowledge, the passion of your employees. What can you do to set yourself apart from your competitors?

3: Beat the Deadlines You Establish

Consumers these days are so used to being let down. We've all been there—we're told a package will arrive Tuesday, but it shows up on Thursday. Make beating deadlines an important part of your organizational culture. Your customers will notice and appreciate it.

4: Provide Exceptional Customer Service

One of the best ways to build a loyal customer base is by consistently providing excellent service. Every business screws up from time to time—when you do so, it's important to do whatever it takes to fix the situation for your customers and clients. When you consider the dismal state of customer service today, particularly on the part of national corporations, you realize that offering exceptional service is a fantastic way to differentiate yourself from the competition and build customer loyalty.

Avoid These Mistakes!

As with any endeavor in which you're ill-equipped to handle on your own (let's be honest—you didn't learn about marketing or business development in law school), there are several mistakes that business owners and lawyers often make when running the marketing for their firm. Here are a few of the biggest mistakes we've seen:

1: There Are No Defined Objectives

The vast majority of lawyers we've spoken with don't have a written marketing plan. Many of them haven't even given serious thought to their marketing, let alone taken the time to define their objectives and map out a path for achieving them. **You need to have objectives.** The more specific, the better.

How many new clients/cases do you need per month? How many consultations must you schedule to earn that business? Where are those consultations going to come from—referrals, networking, internet advertising, direct mail, radio? If you don't have a plan, you're drifting aimlessly. We'll talk more about developing a plan in the next chapter.

2: There Are No Analytics

What's working and what's not working with regards to your marketing? Can you even answer that question? For a lot of lawyers, the honest answer is no. You're investing time and money into marketing and business development, so it's critical that you're measuring success in each area.

Over time, this allows you to refine your strategy—to invest resources into campaigns that are working and to cut your losses when things aren't working. One of the biggest lessons you'll learn in marketing is that everything doesn't play out the way you expect it to. Some of the ideas that you think are brilliant don't pan out. Other ideas perform far better than you would have expected. The only way you can truly understand your marketing performance is by tracking it and adjusting accordingly.

3: You Miss Out on "Low Hanging Fruit"

We see this all the time—lawyers want to jump straight to advanced, expensive, and speculative marketing campaigns before they've mastered the fundamentals. The best example is referrals. The average attorney is only receiving about ⅓ of the referrals they could be receiving from people they already know. Closing that referral gap is a huge deal—imagine doubling or tripling your referrals!

And it's not hard to make it happen—a regular e-newsletter and an effective social media presence make a huge difference. Unfortunately a lot of lawyers would rather talk about SEO or other speculative lead generating strategies that may or may not work even though they don't fully understand them. There's obviously nothing wrong with creative and sophisticated marketing—but start with the basics, and expand from there!

4: There Are No Systems in Place

A consistent flow of new business requires consistent marketing—and that means you need to put systems in place. Many lawyers tend to do their marketing in random spurts, and it's usually panic-based when they realize that their pipeline has dried up.

To avoid the "boom and bust" cycle, it's important to create systems and to work with your team and your outside partners to ensure that the systems are being executed. Whether it's social media, your e-newsletter, your networking strategy, blogging, PR, or whatever else it may be—put systems in place to make sure they're happening consistently. Otherwise, it won't happen.

5: You Have "Bright Shiny Object" Syndrome

This is similar to #3 above. Don't get distracted by the latest buzzwords or ideas that you hear about at conferences or online. There is certainly value in continuing to innovate and to learn, but what tends to happen is that attorneys get excited about something new, so they abandon what they've been doing, even if it's working.

Part of this is a desire for a "magic bullet" that is going to be the solution to all of their challenges. Part of it is human nature—we all tend to get excited about new things. But if you're constantly chasing that bright shiny object, it's easy to lose sight of the big picture. Trust the plan you've created. Pay attention to your analytics so you know what's working and what's not. Innovation is great, but not at the expense of consistent performance!

Chapter 3 ~ Branding vs. Marketing

As if we hadn't front-loaded this book with a lot of bad news, here's something else to consider: Not only do lawyers have an image problem, they have a market problem. In other words, you're becoming a commodity.

For centuries, attorneys enjoyed a prominent role in society. Recognized for their intelligence, discernment, and education, attorneys commanded respect and were able to enjoy a high standard of living in recognition of their contribution to a healthy and just society.

Today, the legal profession is dramatically changing. High levels of competition combined with rapid changes in technology have created unprecedented market conditions. Not only are there more practicing attorneys in the United States than ever before, but the emergence of DIY legal services such as LegalZoom and Rocket Lawyer have created extremely low-cost (or even free) legal solutions for many consumers.

Additionally, these companies also offer services that make it possible for consumers to get a lawyer on retainer and pay as little as $32 for a 30-minute conversation. It's like Uber—but instead of a car and driver, the app connects consumers with a lawyer.

And if that wasn't enough, there's another major shift on the horizon—the emergence of artificial intelligence as a threat not only to low-skill jobs, but also to highly-educated professionals such as accountants, doctors, and yes, even lawyers.

These changes have been years or even decades in the making, but the pace of change is increasing. Combine these forces with the skyrocketing cost of law school, staggering amounts of student loan debt, and the over-saturation of lawyers in many markets, and there's plenty of cause for alarm.

Unfortunately, most of these forces are beyond your control. There's not much you can do to stop change from arriving. What you can control is your response. And believe it or not, there's an opportunity presenting itself in the midst of this rapid evolution. Most lawyers react to these market forces by panicking, lowering their rates, chasing any potential client with a pulse, and essentially **becoming a commodity**.

That's the opposite of what you should be doing. Instead you should be building a brand for yourself as an expert in your practice area and finding ways to create value for your clients above and beyond what they'll find elsewhere. If you allow yourself to become a commodity, you're at the mercy of market forces—and as you already know, that's not a safe place to be right now. Instead, your goal should be to build a brand for yourself that sets you apart from the other lawyers and legal providers that are crowding the market.

This requires a different mindset, and the first step is to accept the reality that a significant percentage of potential clients out there, perhaps even the majority, are always going to choose the cheapest solution—DIY online solutions if possible—and if they're forced to hire a real attorney, they'll pick the absolute cheapest guy in town.

Do not chase those clients.

It's a race you can't win. There will always be someone willing to work for less. And if you attempt to play this game, you'll end up over-worked and miserable because you're not making enough money to enjoy a comfortable lifestyle, let alone hire the staff you need to create a thriving and sustainable practice.

Instead, commit to building a brand and a reputation that positions you as the go-to attorney in your market. When you establish your brand as a leading expert and find a way to provide unique value to your clientele, price becomes much less important because you're not a replaceable commodity anymore. You'll earn more referrals and clients will begin to seek you out, rather than the other way around.

Branding Should Come First

There is an ongoing debate about the role branding should play in a small businesses marketing plan. Proponents of direct marketing often argue that branding is a waste of time and money for a small business—that 100% of a marketing budget should be devoted to trackable lead generation campaigns. Conversely, branding experts argue that without creating and publicizing an appealing image, other marketing efforts will not be effective.

The truth lies somewhere in between.

It is almost always a mistake for a small business to invest into a major branding campaign—such as a TV commercial or a billboard campaign. This type of mass-media advertising doesn't generate results overnight—it takes repeated exposure over a long period of time to have an impact. And such a campaign requires far more cash than most small business owners are willing to invest into their marketing.

On the other hand, direct marketing (such as newspaper advertising, sales letters, online lead generation campaigns, etc.) is far more effective when coupled with a powerful brand. A well-constructed brand defines and strengthens the position of a business within its market.

So what is the proper balance between branding and direct marketing?

Branding should come first. Once you've created and established a strong brand identity, then you focus on direct marketing. Specifically, that means an effective logo and tagline, materials such as business cards and stationery, and a branded website. Creating these basic brand elements allows every direct marketing campaign that follows to reflect a strong, cohesive brand.

Once you have a memorable brand identity that differentiates your business from the competition, you can move on to direct marketing. But until then, your direct marketing campaigns won't have the appeal that they need to maximize your response rate.

Narrow Your Focus

Here's a business paradox for you: The less you do, the more money you'll make.

We're talking specifically about practice areas and the services you provide. Most attorneys don't limit their practice much—you likely know plenty of lawyers who practice family law, estate planning, and business law, along with some criminal defense on the side. Maybe you're one of them.

It's easy to understand why. We're all trying to grow our business, win new clients, and drive revenue. So it's logical to create as broad a practice as possible—to cast the widest net you can to appeal to the largest number of people in some way.

Unfortunately, it doesn't work that way. In fact, building a "generalist" legal practice is going to cap your potential income significantly. Why? **Because we all want to work with an expert**—whether that's hiring a CPA to help with our taxes, a private music teacher for our kids, or a real estate agent to sell our home.

Focusing in on a single practice area, or at least a group of related practice areas, is a critical step to building a powerful brand identity and differentiating yourself from the competition. You cannot and will not be perceived as an expert if your focus is too broad. You've heard the phrase "jack of all trades, master of none." It's very relevant here. Your market needs to know what you're exceptional at, and that's why your focus should narrow.

Most lawyers are very resistant to narrowing their practice areas, often for economic reasons. But keep this in mind: You can start by simply narrowing the focus of your marketing—you don't actually have to turn down clients in other practice areas. We all have bills to pay and you may not be ready to turn down paying clients yet. You can continue to take work in other areas, even as you focus your marketing on a specific niche.

With time, as you focus your marketing and build a brand as a leader in your area of practice, you'll attract more of the work you prefer to do, you'll be able to charge higher rates to do it, and you'll build a much more sustainable and efficient practice because you won't have to reinvent the wheel every time you get a new client.

Narrowing your focus will also make a huge difference when it comes to generating referrals because focusing on a single practice area makes it easy for your network to remember what you do and recognize opportunities to send you work. Not to mention that people are much more likely to refer a lawyer who is an expert in a particular area of need. After all, which sounds better, "Legal Expert" or "Business Law Expert"?

It might seem counterintuitive at first. It might even sound scary. But if you're serious about creating a strong brand to help you stand out from the competition and build a more profitable practice, you need to narrow your focus.

Creating Your Brand

Everyone has a brand. It's not optional. That's because your brand, at its most basic level, is **how you are perceived by the outside world**. So unless you've managed to go through your entire life without making anyone aware of your existence, you've built a brand. The question is: what is your brand, and is it helping you make money?

A brand that positions you as the go-to expert *will* make you more profitable. This happens because when you're perceived as the expert, clients seek you out rather than the other way around. You have the ability to charge higher rates because you've flipped the supply-demand equation in your favor. When you're a "generalist," just one of many interchangeable lawyers, potential clients have options—there's an endless supply. If you become THE go-to attorney—now you've restricted supply because there's only one of you. You'll have clients seeking you out, and basic economics dictates that you can charge premium rates.

So let's talk about how to get there.

It all starts with assessing your brand as it presently exists. You probably have some ideas, but it's very difficult to be objective about yourself. Sure, you know what you think your brand is or what you think people perceive of you, but you really can't be certain unless you ask.

<u>Action Item:</u> Figure Out Your Brand

Open your email inbox and compose an email to trusted friends, colleagues, and clients. Ask the following questions:

1. What words come to mind when you think about me?
2. What are my strengths?
3. What makes me unique?
4. If you had to describe me to someone in one sentence, what would it be?

Are you uncomfortable asking those questions? It's understandable because none of us like to feel vulnerable. But if you explain that you're looking for honest feedback because you're trying to build on your strengths to provide even better service to your clients, most people will be happy to oblige you. And the responses might surprise you. Often, you'll discover strengths and positive traits about yourself that you didn't know existed.

Don't let the fear of potentially negative feedback get in your way. Write up the email and hit "Send."

After you've established what your brand really is, it's time to define your goal. What does your ideal brand look like? How do you want to be perceived? This requires strategic thought. Remember, the more focused your brand is, the more success you'll have at positioning yourself as the best at what you do. Questions to consider are:

What kind of work do you enjoy doing? Your brand has to be authentic—don't chase the dollar signs, because even if you can fake it for a time, sooner or later you're going to burn out if you hate your work.

Where is there an underserved market or an unmet need? This requires some market research, and it's important to be realistic. If there are already established competitors who have built premium brands for themselves in the niche you're considering, it's important to be honest with yourself and understand that you're going to have an uphill battle at first. In this case, you need a strategy to differentiate yourself from those competitors.

What are the traits and attributes that this market values? What are potential clients in your chosen niche looking for in a lawyer? Convenience? Flexibility? Stability? Innovation? Concierge-level client service? Efficiency?

How can you leverage my unique strengths and abilities to serve this market well? Where do your strengths mesh with what the market is looking for? If the market wants stability and you've been in business for 20 years, focus on that. If the market wants convenience and you make yourself available 24/7, that's the direction you go.

Keep in mind that this is not a five minute exercise—it takes time and strategic thought. If you need to put this book down and come back in a couple of weeks once you figure it out, then so be it. But answer those four questions and you'll have a rough sketch of the brand you want to build. After all, you'll have identified an area of focus that you're passionate about that has an unmet need (or at least, a need that you can meet differently), and you have an idea of how to structure your brand to appeal to this market.

Now, how do you make it happen?

Here is an example of a brand identity for a law practice: We want to be perceived as the go-to divorce team for high-net-worth women in Pittsburgh, Pennsylvania. We balance tenacity in the courtroom with empathy and compassion for women going through a life-changing divorce. We understand the emotional turmoil you're feeling, we understand how high the stakes are, and we will fight hard to protect your kids and your lifestyle.

In this statement, we've defined a narrow target market and zeroed in on the marketing message that will differentiate our fictional firm from the thousands of other attorneys in Pittsburgh.

Once you have your brand identity in place, you need to filter all of your marketing and communications through that prism. This includes your website, your social media presence, your networking elevator pitch, and all other marketing materials. Everything from the photos on your website, to the font selection in your brochure, to the layout of your business cards should be selected with your brand objectives in mind.

This is a massive undertaking, but that's what it takes. Invest the time necessary to bring your marketing and communication channels into alignment with the brand you're seeking to create.

Next, take steps to create credibility in your specific niche. In our fictional example, we would encourage the lawyers in the firm to consider:

• Launching a blog specifically focused on providing information and resources to high-net worth women contemplating divorce
• Focusing their social media presence on the same message
• Writing articles for local publications that target their demographic
• Gaining media exposure on the radio and on TV—for example, becoming a recognized commentator on celebrity divorce
• Launching a podcast
• Holding regular events for women—from informational lunch-n-learn style events to relaxing spa days for clients
• Looking for speaking opportunities with groups and organizations that target their demographic
• Publishing a book focused on helping women prepare for and recover from divorce

Again, this won't happen overnight, and it can be hard to accomplish any of this when you're busy with the day-to-day work of serving clients and running your practice. But it's worth dedicating a few hours to create a strategic plan for your branding and marketing efforts.

As you begin to demonstrate your credibility, the next step is to start leveraging your authority within your marketing communications. Feature your podcast prominently on your website. If you've appeared on TV or on the radio, promote your appearances on your social media channels. Create a promotional campaign to celebrate your book launch. Feature magazine articles you've written in your office and in your reception area.

Over time, this is how you take control of your brand and turn it into a profitable tool for your law practice. The bottom line is that you're facing a lot of competition out there—and your brand can be your "secret weapon" that allows you to stand out from the crowd and earn a great living. Don't feel pressured to accomplish all of this quickly. Instead, focus on creating a plan and then taking steps (they can be baby steps!) towards your objective.

Create a Marketing Plan

Once you have your brand identity established and you know who you are as an attorney and law firm, it's time to make a plan for marketing that brand. Effective marketing isn't easy—and there are plenty of ways to waste your time and your resources. This is particularly true for small business owners, as most of us can't afford to spend hours each day refining our marketing tactics. That said, there is one specific mistake that stands out above all the rest: **The failure to have a plan.**

Without a marketing plan, you are flying blind. Your initiatives may seem like a great idea, but with no unifying central purpose, you'll find it impossible to achieve the long-term results that you're looking for.

The good news, however, is that creating an effective marketing plan is easier than you may think. You may associate the term with a 50-page academic paper that a professor made you create during your undergraduate career—but that's not what we are talking about here. A marketing plan can be as small as a single page, but there is no doubt about how important it is as a guide for your overall marketing efforts and, ultimately, your firm's success.

Answer these questions, and you've taken the essential first steps to creating an effective plan.

<u>Action Item:</u> Create a Marketing Plan

At this point, it's time to take everything you've learned so far and put it into place. Start by asking yourself some of the questions we've covered so far, such as:

• **What makes your business different from the competition?** Is it your years of experience? Your use of technology? Your ability to keep costs low?

• **What is your firm's brand?** How do you want your audience to perceive your business?

• **What are the benefits your products and services provide?** Why should a consumer choose your products or services over those of a competitor? What's in it for them?

• **Who is your target market?** Are you selling to businesses or consumers? To locals in your city or to people all over the country? Men or women? And so on.

• **What are the most effective channels to reach your market?** Now that you've defined your audience, how can you best engage them? Internet marketing? Social media? Direct mail? Print advertising?

Once you have a marketing plan written down, figure out the goals you want to achieve and reverse engineer what it will take to achieve them. Those answers shape the marketing you want to do, the goals provide the finish line for your ultimate achievement.

For example, if you want to make $1 million in revenue next year, figure out how many clients you'll need, how many consultations you'll need to have, and how many leads/referrals you'll need to generate. From there, you can use the answers to wrote down to the questions above to begin exploring and implementing the marketing initiatives that will drive you toward achieving that goal.

Chapter 4 ~ It's a Trap!

There are many mistakes you can make in the marketing world, whether it's with your messaging, the campaigns you run, or the vendors you work with that promised you the world. However, the biggest trap you as an attorney can fall into is feeling as though you need to compete on price with everyone else on Google.

As we pointed out in the previous chapter, the legal industry is highly competitive and becoming more so every day. There are more lawyers practicing than ever before, and the popularity of free or dirt-cheap online services like LegalZoom means there's tremendous pressure to lower prices and conform to the demands of the market.

If you're hoping to build a profitable, sustainable practice that provides a great living for yourself and your family, this is obviously a cause for concern. But here's the good news: there's an opportunity created by these market forces that you can exploit. You just have to do things differently than most of the other solo/small firms out there who are responding to these market forces by cutting rates, offering poor client-service, cutting expenses, and generally racing for the bottom.

Prospering in these conditions requires a mindset shift. It requires you to accept the fact that there are many consumers and businesses out there—perhaps even a majority—who will choose the low-cost provider every time. You don't have to chase after those clients. Instead, focus your marketing efforts on a market segment who can and will pay premium rates because they recognize the superior value you are providing.

There are hugely profitable businesses in every industry that charge premium rates and still win business despite the availability of free or lower-cost alternatives. For example, did you know there is such a thing as an oxygen bar? Even though breathable air is literally all around us at all times, there has been a rise in oxygen bars—establishments where you can easily pay $60 an hour or more to breathe pure oxygen, which offers no actual health benefits compared to "normal" air according to medical professionals.

Regardless, customers are lining up to pay for it, despite being literally surrounded by a free alternative. It's an extreme example but hopefully you can see the point. (The bottled water industry is another great example.) If an entire industry can thrive by selling air—readily available for free everywhere around us—at high prices, there's no reason for you to panic when you hear about low-cost competitors. You just need a strategy to attract the right clientele—people who have the means to pay your rates and who see the value in doing so.

The Best Clients Don't Come from Google!

We can't tell you how many conversations we've had with attorneys where the first question they asked was: *"How can I get on the first page of Google?"*

Most lawyers are way too focused on SEO and as a result, they are missing out on bigger and better marketing opportunities. We passionately believe that there is more to the internet than Google. There are more important, more foundational, and more profitable strategies to pursue with your internet marketing.

Most of the potential clients who find your website on Google are transaction-minded. They're price shopping. If you make it to the top of the first page, congratulations, you're going to get a phone call. The problem is, that person is going to call your firm, and then they're going to call 3-4 more firms.

And do you know who they're going to hire? The cheapest option they can find!

When you play the Google game—when you rely on searches for your new clients—you're allowing yourself to become a commodity. If someone searches for "divorce lawyer Atlanta," they get hundreds of results. Most searchers will take a look at those results, call a handful of them, and hire the cheapest option available. In many cases, searchers will make the phone call *without even visiting your website* because even Google knows what the end game is. So when you take that route with your marketing, you have virtually no opportunity to differentiate yourself from the competition.

The best clients don't find you by searching for "bankruptcy lawyer," or whatever your practice is. They seek YOU out by name because of the brand and the reputation YOU have created. Most of the time, this doesn't even happen on Google. It happens through referrals and repeat business. It happens because you've created an unforgettable brand that positions you as the leading expert in your market.

Your main goal shouldn't be to show up at the top of Google's rankings. Your goal should be to become known as THE leader, the go-to lawyer, and the authority in your market. You want prospective clients searching for YOU, not generic search engine phrases.

Those are the clients who are willing to pay premium rates. Those are the clients that come into the engagement pre-conditioned to trust you. They're more likely to treat you and your staff with the respect you deserve, more likely to be loyal for the long-term, and more likely to make referrals of their own.

Chapter 5 ~ Don't Neglect the Real World

You have your brand identity and you have a marketing plan in place. However, you're still not ready to establish an online presence that truly reflects your brand and have it see the success you truly want. Despite what teenagers think, you have to establish a presence in the real world before you can create an effective online presence. This includes your digital marketing ecosystem.

Unfortunately, we don't just mean leasing an office space and putting a sign out by the road. You have to network. You have to put a face to the logo and meet people.

One of our most successful clients started his business law firm from scratch in Miami, which arguably has the highest number of lawyers per capita than anywhere in the country. He had to figure out how to establish himself as an equal to or better than all the other established firms in the city.

Without much of a marketing budget, this client networked constantly. He met as many business owners and potential referral sources as he could and supplanted himself as the go-to attorney if any of them ever needed help. Even though networking isn't as sexy as a new digital marketing campaign, it's a tried-and-true marketing technique that still works.

The Value of Networking

Networking is a critical piece of the business development puzzle for just about every lawyer. Referrals are arguably the very best source of new business—and an active, engaged network is critical to generating those referrals. Additionally, for lawyers still in the "*I have more time than money*" phase of growing their firm, networking is even more crucial.

Unfortunately, it's easy to waste your time. You need a networking *strategy* to ensure that you're investing your time wisely and that you're getting the best possible results from your effort. Here are a few ways to make that happen:

1: Prioritize Quality Over Quantity

Just because there's a networking event near you doesn't mean you need to be there. There are endless opportunities to get out, meet people, and exchange business cards. But the odds of developing even one profitable relationship out of a randomly selected networking event aren't good.

Instead, you need to identify your ideal clients and referral sources and focus your efforts on events and organizations where they congregate. And then, even within those carefully targeted spaces, don't try to meet everyone in the room. Superficial, 30-second conversations and handing out a business card doesn't lead to meaningful relationships. Instead, look to have real conversations with a smaller number of people. When you get to know them and vice versa, you've laid the groundwork for a mutually beneficial relationship.

2: Educate Them

One of your goals as you're conversing with people early in your relationship must be to educate them about what you do, who you help, what makes you different, and what a good referral looks like. It doesn't matter how well you connected with them, if they don't have this information, they're not equipped to send you business.

A sharp elevator pitch is invaluable in this process. Now, understand that you need to perform a balancing act here, because if you make the main focus of the conversation how THEY can help YOU, they're not going to appreciate it. Your goal should be to listen more than you speak and to look for ways to provide value to them. Throughout that process, make sure you've educated them on what you do and what you're trying to do.

3: Be Yourself

As you educate people, don't try to be someone you're not. Show up as yourself with an open mind and a smile. People are more likely to remember you if they are able to make a personal connection with you.

4: Give Before You Get

Don't expect overnight results from your networking efforts. In fact, you should proactively look for opportunities to make the first move. This might mean sending them a referral. It might mean a strategic introduction to someone else in your network that opens doors. It could even mean sending them a gift, a handwritten note, or simply emailing them an article that you think they'll appreciate.

5: Don't Let Yourself Become a Distant Memory

It does not matter how well you connected with an individual, if you give them enough time to do so, they are going to forget about you. That's why it's so important to follow up! This is where most lawyers go wrong, and it's the single biggest opportunity to significantly improve the results of your networking strategy.

We're all busy people, bombarded with distractions, challenges, opportunities and ideas. Meeting a potential referral source and having a great conversation with him/her is *the beginning of this process*, not the end. Networking is nurturing, and simply talking to someone once is never going to be good enough.

You should follow up personally. But as your contact list grows, it's not feasible to personally touch base with everyone in your network multiple times each month. That's where a systematized, scalable strategy is critical. Two simple ways to do this are with your email newsletter and on social media (which will be discussed in depth later). Everyone you meet should be added to your email list—ensuring they hear from you on a regular basis and are constantly reminded and re-educated about your practice. You should encourage them to connect with you on LinkedIn, Twitter, Facebook, or wherever you're most active on social media. This strategy creates regular touch-points and creates top-of-mind awareness in a scalable, sustainable way.

Networking Ideas You Can Use Today

Whether you're a seasoned networker or you've never even thought to go to your local Chamber of Commerce or mixer, here are several tips and ideas you can implement to take your networking strategy and system to the next level. Best of all, there are several things you can delegate or do with your office staff!

1: Social Media Networking

Having a foot in the digital space is a great way to connect with others and expose your brand to a larger audience. Using whichever social media platforms you prefer, connect with your community (other surrounding businesses, local organizations, etc...) and connect with other professionals within your industry. Follow, say hello, share, and engage!

Some platforms like LinkedIn and Facebook have specific groups and forums that you can join as well. This is a great opportunity to see what others within your profession are doing and provides you with opportunities to get involved with other community happenings.

2: Guest Blogging

Do you know of another professional that has a blog? Offer to provide a guest article for them to publish, perhaps in exchange for publishing one of their blogs to your network. It's a win-win! Your brand and content gains exposure to a larger audience and you are helping another professional do the same.

Make sure the topic is relevant to something that you both do. For example, if this person handles divorce cases and you practice estate planning, consider writing a blog about how divorce can affect estate plans.

3: Joining Industry-Specific Organizations

Do some research and find both local and national organizations that you can be a part of. Bar associations are a great place to start. This is a great way to meet new people and make connections. When choosing an organization to join, consider your big-picture goals, your specific client needs, what you want to gain from the organization, the cost to join, the time investment, and the size.

4: Attending Conferences, Classes, and Workshops

These types of gatherings are great for polishing your skills, getting inspired, networking with other professionals, and connecting with potential clients or referral sources. Also, look for opportunities to be a leader or speaker in these types of events. You may not feel like you have a lot to offer, but you do. Share your knowledge, your processes, and your opinions on how you run your own business, or how potential clients could gain benefit from using your services.

5: Volunteering in the Community

This is something that you can do as an individual or even as an entire company or group. Get involved in your surrounding community in a way that benefits others. This is an incredible and humbling way to get your name out there and connect with the everyday people that are in your area that might need your services. Be visible, make personal connections, and let your actions show people what your brand is all about—helping others!

6: Attending a Meet-Up

Believe it or not, there is a huge community of people wanting to meet up for coffee once a week or a happy hour once a month—sometimes with a specific goal in mind, and sometimes just to meet new people and make connections. These may just be random people within your area, or maybe other legal professionals, small business owners, and entrepreneurs.

You don't have to attend a meet-up with the intention of handing out your business card and giving your sales pitch to everyone you come in contact with. There are meet-ups designed for networking purposes specifically, and there are others for people with common interests or the same hobbies. The point of a meet-up is to MEET others. Remember, networking is about nurturing relationships, which doesn't necessarily need to be a business relationship. You never know who may know a friend of a friend that needs your service a month or two down the road!

7: Getting Involved with a Charity

Similar to volunteering, getting involved or helping out a charity is a great way to gain positive brand exposure while giving back! Maybe your office decides to host a canned food drive. Advertise on social media, in your newsletter, and on your website! Share flyers with local businesses, put up a poster on your street, spread the word! The possibilities for giving back are endless, and your firm is sure to stay memorable.

Create an Exceptional Experience

What type of experience do you create for your clients?

As the owner of a law firm (or a business of any kind), it's easy to become so consumed with your own point of view that you never really stop to think about what your clients experience before, during, and after an engagement. However, the client experience you create plays a critical role in the growth of your business.

Do you create "raving fans" that are so blown away by their experience with your law firm that they can't wait to recommend you to others? Do you create a mediocre experience—not great, not terrible, not memorable? Or do clients walk away underwhelmed or downright unhappy with the engagement?

Client experience matters. This is not about creating warm fuzzy feelings—it's about creating clients and customers for life. It's about driving referrals. It's about creating ambassadors for your law firm that spread the word everywhere they go.

Today's customers are highly sensitive to the experience they have while doing business. As a result, businesses that provide an exceptional experience wrapped around their products and services have a huge competitive advantage.

For example, Starbucks can charge $5 for a coffee that would cost you $2 at a coffee stand or 25 cents to make at home. They're selling more than coffee—they're selling the experience of a third place between home and work for their customers to socialize, work, study, or relax. In the 1990s when the company began to grow explosively, this was a brand new concept. The experience they created fueled incredible growth, created customer loyalty, and justified significantly higher price points.

Admission to Disney's Magic Kingdom can be in the ballpark of $150 during peak season. Meanwhile, thousands of amusement parks around the country charge between $40–$60 during peak season. In many cases, these other amusement parks are larger and have a greater variety of rides and attractions. But nobody creates a better experience than Disney. Their attention to detail is unparalleled.

Need proof? Every night, their crew repaints the entrance gate to the park so the next day's visitors see a glistening white coat of paint. Every single night. And, it's a detail that most visitors probably won't consciously recognize. But Disney knows how to create a memorable experience every step of the way, and that's why they can charge two or three times the rate of local amusement parks and still draw tens of millions of visitors from across the world each year.

The Mayo Clinic has differentiated themselves in the medical field by focusing on their patient experience. For example, their standard hospital rooms are larger than the industry average and contain more amenities. They've placed couches in doctors' offices to help patients relax and feel more comfortable. They enforce a strict dress code for doctors while meeting with patients.

They don't keep patients waiting when they've got an appointment. Management is known to ask employees to replace their shoelaces if they're dirty. Their attention to detail communicates respect and appreciation to their patients, and it has powerfully differentiated Mayo from other healthcare providers to the point that patients will often travel significant distances and pay more money to be treated at Mayo rather than a local provider.

So how does this apply to your law firm?

Obviously, providing a great experience doesn't replace the need for quality legal work. None of the examples above would be sustainable if the actual products and services those businesses provided weren't acceptable. But if you can engineer an exceptional client experience wrapped around the work you provide, you're pouring rocket fuel into your business development process. Clients who have an excellent experience become ambassadors for your firm and refer people your way every chance they get. You'll have the ability to charge above-market rates and still win business. Your staff will be more motivated and bought-in to your mission.

If you're having trouble wrapping your head around this, think about your own experience as a consumer. When have you had an experience that surpassed your expectations and how did that change the way you felt about the establishment?

So how do you implement an exceptional customer experience in your firm?

The first thing to consider is what an ideal experience looks like for your target market. There's no one-size-fits-all solution here. High net-worth clients who are planning for the future of their estate are looking for a much different experience than an individual facing criminal charges. But here are some things to consider:

• **Your office decor, layout, and amenities:** Is your lobby/waiting room pleasant? Do you have drinks available? Is it self-serve, or does your staff actually serve them?

• **Your office location:** Are you located in an area that your target clients want to visit?

• **Your physical appearance:** Many lawyers don't dress as formally as they did 10 or 20 years ago. And that can be just fine—but whatever your dress code is, make sure you look put-together and professional.

• **The appearance of your staff:** Your team serves on the frontline in client engagements, so it's important that they represent you well. Think about the Mayo Clinic example—the details matter, even down to the shoelaces!

51

• **Your branding.** Think about your website, your logo, your marketing materials – do they represent you in the way you want to be represented? Are they appealing to your target clients?

• **The way your phones are answered.** You should have a script or at least clear guidelines. And please, please, please, if your staff answers the phone and simply says "Law Office," revise it immediately!

• **Client communication policies.** Responding to clients in a timely manner makes a big difference. Make it a point to communicate proactively with clients and help them understand what's going on with their matter.

This list is just the beginning. Take some time to map out your client engagement from start to finish—from their initial phone call, to a consultation, to the legal work itself, to the follow up after the matter is resolved. Pay attention to the details, even down to the shoelaces!

Remember, there's no one-size-fits-all solution here. First and foremost, the client experience you create needs to be customized for your target clients. A good experience for a client going through a divorce is different than a good experience for a client who's launching a new business.

Action Item: Process Audit

Even though it has little to do with your marketing, it has everything to do with your brand. Compare your internal processes to your brand identity. If something doesn't line up for can be improved, revise your policies and procedures (you do have a P&P manual, right?). Use the bulleted list above for guidance, but also make sure you leave no stone unturned. A consistent brand really drives home the message you're broadcasting.

Chapter 6 ~ Your Digital Office Space: The Website

Now that we've covered the initial steps of building your brand, crafting a marketing plan, and getting boots on the ground, let's dive into the elements of the digital ecosystem you need to create in order to establish that premium brand.

It all starts with your website. In today's world, it's more often than not going to make the first impression on behalf of your firm, so it better look good and accurately portray the brand you've created. You need to treat it with the same attention to detail and work that you put into selecting and decorating your physical office—assuming you actually put careful thought into your physical office.

The Benefits of a Great Website

For starters, it makes your sales process easier. You know you technically have a sales department in your law firm, right? It may just consist of you, or perhaps it's a secretary and other staff members, but anyone who fields phone calls from leads and referrals is in sales. Your consultations are also sales.

Prospects, including referrals, should always be encouraged to look at your website before coming in or scheduling a phone appointment. If your website demonstrates your value, credibility, and knowledge to clients, it will make the sales process easier for everyone.

We have had multiple clients acknowledge that they have noticed a difference in their ability to close deals with clients much more easily because they invested in their website. Spending less time having to convince prospects that you are the right person to help them means more time and energy to spend on your practice—or on vacation!

A great website also allows you to charge the rates you want. After all, if prospects perceive you as a credible expert in your field, it increases the likelihood that they will pay you what you are worth. Of course, everyone has a different target market, so at the end of the day it is up to you to determine what you can charge based on your market.

Think of it this way, let's say you are really sick and need to see a doctor. Do you want just any doctor? NO! You want the best you can get, someone who is the perfect fit, and is an expert in curing whatever is ailing you. Your prospects have a need, and if they realize you are the best fit for them, they are usually willing to pay the proper price to get the right solution.

Lastly, a great website should help you increase referrals. When you have a website that helps sell you to prospects, it means you have a website that makes a great first impression. Whether it's a random person who finds you through Google, a colleague you met at a networking event, or the people who are already your clients, all of them should check out your website. If your website makes the right impression on them, they are all the more likely to think of you down the road when they or someone they know has a need.

Of course, this truth applies to all aspects of your marketing and relationships. How you carry yourself at a networking event or how good of a job you do for your clients—these things are very important as well. However, don't sell yourself short of the value of the lasting impression your website can make on people.

Overall, a well-done and strategic website is an integral part of running your firm these days. Make it a priority now to improve your online presence and experience the benefits!

It Starts with the Home Page

Everyone knows that their website needs a home page, but many people aren't sure what that home page should have, look like, and do. Below are several important elements:

1: A Video Introduction
Some people prefer watching a video versus reading text. Providing a video introduction at the top of your home page gives them this

option. It also establishes a more personal connection with your audience, giving them the opportunity to see your face and hear your voice.

2: Concise, Clearly Worded Content

Your home page needs a clear written description of your business and how you can help. It's important that this introduction be written in a language that makes sense to your target audience, not legalese or techno-speak. Focus this text on the *problem* that your target customers have and demonstrate that YOU are the solution.

3: An Easy Way to Get in Touch

If a website visitor wants to get in touch with you, make it easy! Include your firm's phone number and email address in a prominent location, and provide a contact form that a visitor can fill out if they prefer.

4: A Clean, Organized Menu

It's important that your menu is clear and easy to navigate. Don't make it hard for your visitors to find whatever it is that they're looking for. Because you'll likely have more pages on your website than can comfortably fit in your main menu area, you'll need to think hard about which pages are most important to put in the main navigation menu, and which can be located in sub-menus or drop-downs.

5: A Free Download

A practical report, white paper, or e-book is important for at least two reasons. First, even if a visitor doesn't download it, the mere existence of that content proves your expertise. Secondly, if you can create a report that is appealing to website visitors, you can capture their contact information in exchange for the free download. You can then plug them in to your marketing cycle as appropriate.

6: Links to Social Media Profiles

A social media presence is an expectation for today's firms, so make it easy for your visitors to find you. Social media is another great touch point that allows you to stay top-of-mind with your audience (that we'll discuss later), so making it easy for website visitors to connect with you is very valuable.

7: Logo, Firm Name, and Tagline

This sounds obvious, but many firms today don't even have their logo and firm identity on their website. Ten years ago, that may have been okay, but in today's internet-centric age, a professionally designed and well-branded website is very important. It doesn't have to be an artistic masterpiece, but at the very least your home page needs to reflect your brand identity appropriately.

Beyond the Home Page

This is not intended to serve as a complete list of everything your website needs, and not all of these components will apply to every firm website. But each of these elements is very important, and it should be a part of a law firm website in almost every circumstance.

If your website is going to reflect your status and expertise, as well as engage your visitors and help generate new business, it should have the following pages and functionality:

1: Industry Focused, Regularly Updated Blog

A blog is an extremely valuable tool in terms of attracting traffic to your website, engaging your audience, and demonstrating your expertise. Your blog should focus on providing value to your target market—and one of the best ways to do this is to write blog entries addressing common questions and concerns that your market has. This shows your readers that you understand their concerns and that you are well positioned to help them.

2: Testimonials / Success Stories

Studies have conclusively proven that the use of testimonials greatly aids the sales process. Potential customers want to be reassured that you've helped other people like them in the past, and testimonials allow you to do just that. Your testimonials and success stories should be featured prominently on your website as long as your bar association regulations allow you to do so.

3: Contact Page with an Accurate Map

When a website visitor is ready to get in touch with you, make it easy! Your contact page should be easy to find and clearly display your contact information. Include a contact form that can be filled out directly from your site in case the individual doesn't want to call or email. It's also important to have an accurate, easy-to-use map on your contact page for clients who wish to visit your office in person.

4: Services Page That Clearly Explains How You Can Help

It's important that website visitors immediately understand what you do. A services page is a great place to do this. While creating the content for this page, don't use confusing legal or technical jargon. Instead, take your services and translate them into clear, direct language that will resonate with your market.

5: Lead Capture Forms on Every Page

One of the primary purposes of your website is to convert prospects and help you grow your practice. To do so, use lead capture forms on every page of your site. This can be as simple as a box on your sidebar encouraging your readers to download content such as a special report in exchange for their contact information.

Your Content Is Important!

The actual written text of your website deserves just as much attention as the visuals. Your website is an opportunity to tell your story, connect with prospects and potential referral sources, and build your credibility. Your website content plays a significant role in this.

Unfortunately, many lawyers don't give their website content enough attention. They often read like a glorified resume:

- *"Bob graduated from law school in 1995."*
- *"Susan is a member of the American Bar Association and serves on the family law advisory board of the Chicago Bar Association."*
- *"Sam won the Most Likely to Succeed award at the Temple University Beasley School of Law."*

No offense, but most of your clients and potential clients don't care about the awards you won in law school. There's room in your website content to cover accolades and accomplishments, but with very few exceptions. They should not be front and center.

The first step in writing strong website content for your law firm is to **shift your focus from yourself to your audience**. Your website isn't a place to congratulate yourself. It's a place to *connect with your audience*, to show them that you *understand their challenges*, and that you actually care about *helping your clients* improve their lives.

It requires the right mindset. The key is to place yourself in the shoes of your target market and ask yourself: *"What do THEY want and need to read on my website?"*

Here are four ways to accomplish this:

1: Quickly and Clearly Identify What You Do and Who You Do It For

It's very obvious to YOU what you do and what kind of clients you work with, but it's not at all obvious to your website visitors if you don't spell it out for them. Use headlines and home page copy to clearly spell out what you do and what type of clients you work with. This lets your ideal clients know that they are in the right place. If website visitors can't tell what you do within a couple of seconds of opening your site, you're not doing a good enough job with your communication.

2: Don't Over-Emphasize Your Resume

Prospective clients aren't as interested in your resume and your accomplishments as you are. The pressing question for them is "*can you help me?*" Don't devote prime real estate on your website to your resume unless there are very specific and significant reasons why this information should be highlighted. Instead…

3: Show Your Audience That You Get It

Empathize with your target market. Show them that you understand their fears. If you're a family lawyer, let readers know that you understand the emotional turmoil they are facing. If you're a tax defense attorney, make it clear that you understand how freaked out your prospects are to have the IRS on their case. If you do criminal defense, acknowledge that your potential clients are gearing up for the fight of their life. Your prospects want to know that their attorney understands what they are going through, so don't be afraid to acknowledge the emotions that your clients are experiencing and show them that you get it.

4: Minimize the Legalese

You're a lawyer and you likely spend a lot of time with other lawyers. Your clients, however, are not lawyers, and if you write your website content as if they were, it's not going to resonate. Tone down the technical language and write in the language of your target market. Website content for an estate planning firm that targets high net worth individuals should look very different from a foreclosure defense firm's website. Write for your target market, not your friends, your colleagues, or your law professor.

You Need a Free Resource

Offering a download on your law firm website—available to visitors for free in exchange for their email address—is a big opportunity that many lawyers aren't taking advantage of. It's a secret weapon that you can deploy to elevate your credibility and establishing your expertise with a visitor. Here are a few reasons why this is a big deal:

1: It Establishes Credibility
When you do research for yourself to find a professional in a certain field, you want to make sure they're credible and knowledgeable. Let's say you're searching for a doctor or mechanic. If their website had a section dedicated to resources and content they had created, it would show you that they're an expert on that subject.

When people search for a lawyer, it's normally during a stressful time, and they want to know that they are putting their faith in someone who can efficiently help them and has the expertise and knowledge to get them through a rough time. Creating a free resource and including it on your website proves your expertise.

2: It Captures Contact Information
Offering a free download gives you a chance to capture contact information from potential clients. You're much more likely to persuade someone to give you their contact information if something is in it for them. In exchange for their email address, they'll receive access to the free resource that you have created. It's a win-win situation because now you can add them to your email list, continue to stay in touch with them, and make sure you stay on the top of their mind.

When the need arises for a lawyer, you'll be the first person they call because you've created a system to stay in touch with them. This is a very big deal. Imagine if you had a way to stay in touch with many of your website visitors rather than them being gone forever after they leave your website. That's what your free resource can provide.

3: It Proves That You Care

Lawyers must confront the stereotype that they're in it primarily for the money—not serving clients. Unfortunately, that's a prevailing stereotype among many consumers. And while we know that isn't really the case, that's the reality that must be addressed. By giving away valuable information, you're showing everyone that comes to your website that you care about making sure they are informed whether or not they end up hiring you. This demonstrates your desire to provide help to anyone who needs it, not just those who pay for your services. That goes a long way with potential clients who are on the fence.

So what should this free resource consist of?

There are a variety of options—including infographics, a special report or white paper, or even a video course. The infographic should be informative, but also visually appealing. It could include some answers to frequently asked questions or information about the basic problems that you solve for your clients. A special report or white paper could educate potential clients on what to do if they run into a challenge. For example, if you do personal injury law, you could create a report entitled *"What to Do if You're in a Car Accident: Five First Steps."*

Avoid These Mistakes!

We've seen a lot of attorney websites, and there are many great ones. However, there are A LOT of bad attorney websites out there. If you are the owner of one of those bad websites, it is costing you not only thousands of dollars in lost business, but it's doing damage to your reputation as an attorney.

Your website is like a digital version of your physical office. You likely spent a lot of time carefully thinking about the environment you wanted your office to have, so why wouldn't you do the same for your website? After all, people will almost certainly visit your website before they step foot in your office. If your website looks awful, it tells people your firm is awful, too.

Here are three of the biggest mistakes you could make with your website:

1: Having a Friend Design Your Site

At this point in our technologically advanced society, most of us have a friend or family member who dabbles in web design. It's easy to be tempted to let them handle it, especially if they offer to do it at a discount (or better yet, for free).

But think about this: Would you advise your clients to let their friends or family handle their legal issues at a discount? Of course not! So why do it with your website?

Even if your friend comes up with a good design, there's a good chance they aren't good at coming up with good messaging. A pretty website that doesn't communicate how you help is still a bad website.

2: Cliche Website Designs

If your website contains any of the following images, please stop reading this book and make serious changes:

- The scales of justice
- A gavel
- Your local courthouse steps

People know you're a lawyer. Those images are just acting as a filler and aren't contributing at all. You need powerful images that speak to the needs and emotions of your website's visitors. A gavel doesn't even come close to doing that.

3: Focusing on Yourself

This might sting—but you are not the hero of this story. You didn't spend all those years in school to be a superhero saving the world from traffic tickets, a vengeful spouse, or the IRS.

Instead, you are the guide, helping your client—the real hero—overcome an obstacle. Unfortunately, most attorney websites don't convey this message. You want to appeal to your visitors' emotional needs, not your own ego.

<u>Action Item:</u> The Website Appraisal

Go to your firm's website and grade your site on the criteria below. Reference the scoring key below for information on how to grade yourself:

0: You do not have this item

1: You have this item, but it's difficult to find, missing certain elements, or can otherwise be improved

2: You have this item, it's high quality, and you're getting out of it what you should be

1. Contact Form / Call to Action
2. Free Resources
3. Social Media Links
4. Blog
5. Videos
6. E-newsletter Sign Up
7. Client Testimonials
8. Professional Design
9. Clarity of Services
10. Logo / Branding Prominently Displayed

What did you score on your website appraisal?

0-9: Your website is pretty bad and is doing more harm than good. You're likely missing out on referrals and potential leads. Additionally, your website isn't filtering prospects the way it should be, meaning you're spending too much time with the wrong clients or selling yourself and services. Strongly consider making some big changes.

10-15: Your website is doing a few things right. However, the question is more about where you are missing out. There are elements that can be added or improved upon that would result in a higher conversion rate or higher quality clients (or both). Your website gives prospects some sense as to whether or not you're the right fit for them, but a few improvements could result in more leads, referrals, and overall value per client.

16-20: Congrats! Your website is pretty great. It's helping you create leads, and it's creating referrals. Furthermore, it's positioning you as an expert in your practice area, which results in higher quality prospects coming to your office. Your website is building your brand and credibility, converting website visitors into leads, and educating prospective clients. Even more, your website is enhancing any offline marketing efforts you have in place.

Attract the Right Prospects

Should your law firm website repel visitors, actively discouraging them from contacting your law firm? The answer is YES, which may come as a surprise to you.

Of course, your website should make you extremely attractive to your target market by positioning you as an expert in your area of practice, providing valuable resources, and making it easy to contact you.

But almost as importantly, it should discourage the wrong people from contacting you. You do this gently and subtly of course, but your website and the content on your site should make it clear that you're NOT the right lawyer for people outside of your target market. Here are some examples of the people you should be discouraging from contacting you:

- People who can't afford your rates
- Prospects who need work outside of your areas of focus

- The wrong gender, if applicable—i.e. if you're a divorce attorney focused specifically on women
- Prospective clients who have unrealistic expectations or demands

The list goes on, but hopefully you get the point. You don't want these people contacting you for at least two reasons.

First, because they clog up your intake process. You or someone on your staff has to waste time getting in touch with them, setting up a consultation, and following up only to ultimately find out that they aren't a good fit.

Second, and arguably even worse, because some of them may become nightmare clients. Maybe they can't pay their bill. Maybe they force you to work outside of your area of focus. Maybe they're just jerks.

We understand that it can be hard to turn down work when you have bills to pay, but in the long run doing work you don't want to be doing and working with clients who don't energize you is a sure path to a burnout. It also leads to a weak, diluted brand and position in your market.

That's why it's important that your website serves as a gatekeeper of sorts—making you VERY attractive to your target market, but also making it clear to people outside of your target market that you're not the solution for their needs.

Chapter 7 ~ Your Information Center: The Blog

It's not enough to simply have a website. You need to be consistently adding content to it. This is where your blog comes into play. It's not something millennials do to review restaurants or document their travel experiences, it's how people of all ages find answers to their problems.

It's no different in the legal world. Entrepreneurs need to know what legal documents they need to start a business. Aging adults need to know if a simple Will is adequate for their estate plan. A blog is your website's living, breathing information center. If that isn't convincing enough, here are a few more reasons why you need one:

1: It Engages Visitors

If you create blog content that provides practical information for your website visitors, you're giving them a great reason to linger on your website. For example, if you're a business lawyer, writing a blog entry highlighting the benefits of incorporating as an LLC versus a corporation will be of great interest to at least a portion of your potential clients. Follow it up with a blog entry offering five tips to reduce the chances of being sued and you'll hook another significant portion of your website visitors. The bottom line is that you're giving potential clients a reason to spend time on your website and helping them develop trust and rapport. That way when they are ready to hire a lawyer, you're the one they think of.

2. It Builds Your Expert Status

Not only are you educating and engaging your readers with your blog, you are also establishing yourself as an expert in their mind. Your blog allows you to demonstrate your knowledge and your command of the issues that your clients are concerned about. It also gives you a platform to showcase the type of work you do and the type of clients that you can help.

3: It Creates a Reason for Repeat Visits

If you're regularly adding new content to your blog, you're creating a reason for potential clients to keep coming back to your website. There are potential clients out there for you who are still at the very top of your sales funnel. In other words, they are just beginning to realize their need for a lawyer. They're thinking about their challenge/opportunity and doing their research.

These are the prospects that will come back to your blog regularly if you've made it a source of useful information for them. Then, when they're finally ready to hire a lawyer weeks or months down the road, you've got an inside track because you've already built credibility and established a relationship with them.

4: It Provides Content for You to Feature Elsewhere

Blog entries make for great content to share on social media (which allows you to drive traffic back to your website), through your email newsletter, and across other channels. The key to creating an engaging marketing presence is to provide value to your audience. If you do that through your blog entries, you can leverage the content in countless different areas of your marketing. It's one of the critical engines at the core of all your marketing.

5: It Provides Additional Branding Opportunities

If you blog regularly, you'll soon end up with a whole lot of great content. Now you have the opportunity to repurpose it elsewhere with minimal work required on your part. Hire an editor and have that person turn the blog entries into a book. Stitch two or three entries together into an article and submit it to industry publications. Use your blog entries as a guideline for a podcast. The opportunities are endless.

So what's the downside? Blogging is a lot of work, but you need to make this happen. If you're not ready to hire a professional firm to write your blogs for you, here are two simple ways you can still make it happen:

1: Delegate!

If you have an in-house marketing person, make sure blogging is one of their tasks to complete on a regular basis. It really only has to be monthly. The key is to hold them accountable to make sure it gets done.

2: Do It Yourself

We've lost count of the amount of lawyers who have told us that they really like writing and that they're going to write their blog entries by themselves. We can, however, count on one hand the amount of them who actually did it consistently. You're busy, and blogging isn't going to happen unless you treat it like a non-negotiable task. Put it on your calendar just like you schedule a client meeting or a court appearance and take it just as seriously. This is the only way to make it happen; otherwise, you'll never get around to it.

What Makes an Effective Blog?

Today, it's easy (and free) to get started with a basic blog on a platform such as WordPress. But your blog won't do you a whole lot of good if you don't have a strategy and a plan of attack. Below are six steps to help you blog effectively:

1: Define Your Audience

First and foremost, who is your blog intended to reach? As a consumer protection attorney, for instance, your desired audience may be people who have been deceived by a faulty product. Define your target audience and design your blog to appeal to that audience as much as possible.

2: Write Compelling Headlines

Choosing the right headlines are important, especially when it comes to prompting a potential reader to click on a link to your blog post. Think about your audience and what they want and craft your headlines in a manner that appeals to them as much as possible.

3: Leave Plenty of White Space

If your blog entries look like a wall of text, they won't get read. Instead, use short paragraphs with space in between. If possible, use bold font in order to draw attention to key posts. The goal is to give your readers the ability to quickly scan your post in search of specific information. If they find what they're looking for, chances are that they will take the time to read the whole thing.

4: Provide Actionable Information

Nine times out of ten, when a reader finds your blog it's because they're looking for actionable information. So give it to them! There are plenty of ways to do this. Just be sure to ask yourself this question before you hit the "publish" button: *"Will readers walk away from this post ready and able to take action?"*

5: Write Consistently

Updating your blog every few months simply isn't good enough. You need to update it monthly at the very least so your human readers have a reason to keep coming back. The biggest challenge most lawyers have with this is simply time. It seems like there is always something more important to do. Set aside a specific time in your calendar to work on writing blog content.

Determining Your Blog Topics

Every blog is different and finding out how to sculpt yours can be challenging, but here's the simplest way you can determine what to write about: **Answer the questions your clients ask you on a regular basis.**

If you already have a video FAQ library, this is a great place to start (we'll talk more about videos soon). Take some of the videos and have someone on your team transcribe them into a blog post. While a lot of people prefer watching video, many prefer to read text instead. By answering the same questions across multiple mediums, you'll reach double the audience.

If you still aren't sure which topics to choose, start jotting down questions that your clients ask you. Even though you could rattle off the answers in your sleep because you've been practicing law for years, the people who hire you are most likely new to this situation and aren't sure how to proceed. They are going to have many questions along the way, and many of them are going to be broad and not case-specific. That's where you start building your category of blog topics.

Here are a few examples of blog topics you could use based on different practice areas:

A DUI attorney could write blogs answering questions like:
• What happens if I refuse to take a breathalyzer test?
• Can I get a DUI even if I haven't been drinking?
• Can I be arrested based on someone else's word?

A family lawyer could use a blog to answer these questions:
• If my spouse cheated, how does this affect our divorce?
• What is legally required for the relocation of our children?
• How long is the divorce process in my state?

An Immigration lawyer could write about questions such as:
• What is the difference between a green card and an immigrant visa?
• How can I become a US citizen?
• How can my spouse and I prepare for our marriage interview with USCIS?

An estate planning attorney can write about things like:
• What is the difference between a Will and a trust?
• What type of Power of Attorney do I need?

- What is involved in the probate process?

Regardless of your practice area, there are dozens, if not hundreds, of topics to write about. Once you've decided what to write about, there are still many things to consider: tone, length, structure, etc. However, those things will come together with time. The key is to just start writing and fill up your blog library with articles!

Chapter 8 ~ The Most Underutilized Tool in Your Firm

You have a powerful tool at your disposal right now, and chances are you're not even using it (and if you are, you likely aren't tapping into its full potential). We're talking about your contact list. We understand that email marketing has earned a bad reputation over the years thanks to spammers abusing the system to the point that many of us receive hundreds of unwanted emails each day.

However, a strategic, value-based approach to email marketing can provide a great return for professional firms. According to industry experts, every dollar spent on marketing to your contacts yields a $40 return. Even more, unlike other marketing, your contact list is an asset that you have full control over.

The key is to focus on providing value to your readers—to give them a reason to keep opening your emails, reading them, and clicking your links. To put it plainly: **Not having an e-newsletter for your law firm could be one of the biggest marketing mistakes you can make.** There are more clients and opportunities waiting for you from the people you already know, and an e-newsletter is a simple, yet hugely effective strategy that can help.

If your biggest concern is that people won't want to receive your e-newsletter, they can just unsubscribe. Stop overthinking it!

Here are some more reasons why email should be a core part of your marketing strategy:

1: You Don't Have Enough Time to Stay in Touch With EVERYONE

You hopefully already know how important it is to network and build referral relationships. But, what happens to all the people you meet? Most likely you pick a select few to follow up with. Maybe you even schedule the occasional lunch or coffee meeting. However, there is just not enough time in a given day, week, or even month to stay in touch with everyone you know.

You don't know what business or opportunities you are missing because you can't possibly leverage every relationship you have. Well, with one click of a button you can reach out to everyone you know every month with an e-newsletter. While it's not as effective as a phone call or having lunch, it's a way to stay top-of-mind with every single person you have ever met.

2: You Will Make More Money

We've said it before and we'll say it again—you are only getting about 33% of the referrals that you should be getting from people you already know. Well, that is exactly who your email newsletter is meant for—people you already know. We have heard countless stories of people getting business from someone years after they met, and the only correspondence during that time was their law firm's e-newsletter.

3: You Remind People What You Do

It happens all the time—people don't send you business because they forgot who you are and what you do. To fix that problem, we recommend putting one of your blog articles into your e-newsletter. If your blogs are done correctly, then they communicate what you do and how you help people. That is why featuring a blog in your e-newsletter is a great strategy, because then your e-newsletter not only keeps you in touch with everyone, but it also reminds them what you do.

The bottom line is that an email newsletter for your law firm will keep you in touch with people, make sure they don't forget what you do, and ultimately results in more clients (as well as strategic opportunities and relationships).

Stop making excuses for why you don't need one or why it won't work. Even people who don't open your e-newsletter will still be reminded of you. If you think having a law firm e-newsletter is not for you, you must not like growing your firm. We know that sounds harsh, but you know it's true. Referrals are the best source of business, staying top-of-mind with your contacts is key, and educating referral sources on what you do is paramount. An e-newsletter is a tool that helps you do all of those things.

Building Your Email List

An email newsletter is only as effective as your mailing list. We have clients who have 5,000+ recipients on their list, and every time their newsletter goes out they can pretty much count on a few referrals coming in. We've also had clients who have less than 50 names on their list. As you can imagine, the smaller lists are less effective.

Here's the good news: no matter how small your email list may currently be, there are steps that you can take to grow it dramatically. Below are four ways to make this happen:

1: Export Contacts from Your Email Provider

Practically every email provider, including Outlook, Apple Mail, Gmail, and just about everyone else, makes it very easy to export a list of your contacts. This step alone will typically provide hundreds—if not thousands—of contacts you can add to your distribution list because your email provider records everyone who has ever emailed you. If you haven't already done this, you should do so right now.

2: Go Through Stacks of Business Cards, Past Correspondence, Etc.

If you're like most lawyers, you probably have a desk drawer or a cabinet somewhere in your office that is full of business cards you've collected over the years. These people may be potential clients, referral sources, colleagues, etc. This is a great task to hand off to someone on your team. Simply ask them to create a spreadsheet and record the name and email address from each card.

<u>Action Item:</u> Build Your Contact List

Open a blank spreadsheet and create three columns: First Name, Last Name, and Email Address. Then, complete points 1 and 2 above. This may take some time, especially if you have a ton of business cards lying around.

Once you have that list, go through and delete any sort of "noreply" or auto-generated emails that would obviously kick back if you sent them something. Once you do that, you have your distribution list for an e-newsletter. If your list is several hundred or even thousands of names, you can feel certain that there is five or six figures' worth of business just waiting to be claimed. All you have to do is remind people that you exist and that you can help them.

3: Offer a Giveaway on Your Website

One of the best ways to capture email addresses on an ongoing basis is by providing some sort of resource on your website—such as a white paper, special report, legal guide, or something along those lines. Offer it for free, but require website visitors to provide their name and email address in order to gain access. This is an effective strategy to grow your email list. At the same time, it builds your perception as an expert in your area of practice and it engages and educates potential clients.

4: Make a Habit of Always Adding New Contacts That You Meet While Networking

Whenever you're out networking, make a habit of adding new connections to your list. You can simply hold on to the business cards you collect and give them to someone on your team to input into your spreadsheet. Over time, this practice will dramatically grow your list, even if it's just by 2-3 contacts at a time. This strategy also magnifies the power of your networking. Rather than meeting someone once and then gradually losing track of each other, you now have a system in place to ensure regular communication and maintain top-of-mind awareness.

A Note About Spamming

Many lawyers are concerned about spamming people and are reluctant to add contacts to their distribution list. That's certainly a valid concern, but here are a couple of things to keep in mind. First, if you are doing your e-newsletter right, it is providing value to your recipients. It's not a spammy advertisement. Instead, it's providing them with practical information and ideas that they can use to improve their lives. Second, every reputable e-newsletter provider has a very simple unsubscribe mechanism and includes it in every communication. If your contacts don't want to be on your list, it's easy for them to opt-out.

Key E-Newsletter Strategies

Simply sending an e-newsletter doesn't mean the referrals will start pouring in. There are a lot of wrong ways to send an e-newsletter, which will ultimately send your correspondence straight to the trash. Here are a few things to keep in mind when crafting your e-newsletters:

1: Keep It Short

Email newsletters are not the same as printed newsletters. Printed newsletters are expected to be multiple pages where recipients spend several minutes reading. An e-newsletter, on the other hand, lives within someone's email inbox; thus, there are no pages. People are unlikely to scroll very far, let alone digest a ton of content. Try to limit your e-newsletter to the most important content. Keep in mind if you have something long to share, post it on your website and then just link to it from your e-newsletter.

2: Feature Practical and Helpful Content

We've seen a lot of e-newsletters with useless content. Your e-newsletter ultimately needs to be a tool that helps you grow your firm. It should feature content that helps your audience, but is also related to what you do. For example, putting a cookie recipe in your e-newsletter does nothing to help your firm. However, including a blog that is related to how you help people or a video addressing a common question you get, is something that is both valuable to the recipient and also serves your marketing needs.

3: Include a Personal Touch

Make sure people remember that there are humans behind your law firm. Include a personal introduction in each e-newsletter you send out. The introduction thanks them for reading your e-newsletter and reminds them how they can refer to you should they know someone who needs your help. If you have any news or announcements from the firm, this is a great place to put that.

4: Choose a Subject Line That Works, Even If They Don't Open It

It is a statistical reality that the majority of your email list will actually not open your e-newsletter. First of all, don't be discouraged. There will be enough people that do open it to make it worthwhile. However, the subject line of an email is something everyone will see, even if they don't open your email.

That doesn't mean you should write clickbait headlines just to increase your open rate. Instead, take the title of whatever blog is featured in the e-newsletter and use that as the subject line. This way, everyone at least sees the blog title and is reminded of what you do, even if they don't open the email.

Chapter 9 ~ Stay in Touch with Your Community Through Social Media

As an attorney, you might believe that social media is just something a bunch of millennials are into as a way to avoid making actual interpersonal communication in the real world. But it's so much more than that. Having an active social media presence can go a long way toward building and enhancing your online brand.

The problem is that "social media presence" is an impossibly nebulous term and just deciding that it's "time to get on social media" is so vague that it doesn't really mean anything. In working with attorneys over the last few years, we've heard two different lines of thinking from those who chose to forego any type of social media presence:

"I don't understand it so I don't want it."

Or…

"It's a waste of time because it doesn't generate leads."

Of course you can see the logical flaw in the first example, but what about the second objection? Sure, social media can generate leads. However, you could also generate leads by standing on the side of the highway and holding up a sign with your logo on it. In other words, social media isn't necessarily going to be a big lead magnet for you. But that doesn't mean you shouldn't make it part of your marketing.

The more beneficial approach to social media is to use it as a way to reach people in your community and create a consistent touchpoint with those people, making you a truly unforgettable figure in their lives. You can promote your website and the things you're doing outside of the office to show people that you're not only an expert and the go-to attorney for your practice area, but that you're committed to actually helping people rather than chasing down a big payday.

Social media is a key branding tool because it's an easy way to expose your business to your community with the push of a button. If you're doing an e-newsletter or any kind of direct mail campaign, you can look at social media as a small, daily version of that kind of marketing. Where social media has an advantage, however, is that you can reach your entire community (or the entire country if that's your target market) with your social media content even if you don't have their email, phone number, or physical address.

If your contact list is pretty small, social media allows you to reach the rest of your market. Whether you live in a city of 500,000, or a smaller town of 30,000, social media allows you to reach the people you serve for a fraction of the cost of other forms of marketing. Even though Facebook, social media's biggest platform, has done a lot to curb the influence advertisers like you can have on everyone's timelines, there are still ways you can reach thousands of people in your community every month.

Beyond Facebook, regularly making posts on Twitter and LinkedIn can enhance your brand and give you influencer authority and credibility as *the* expert in your city. From there, the referrals can grow. If a family law attorney needs to send you an estate planning case, a strong social media presence only increases the chances that attorney will think of you first because they've seen your content posted across social media.

How Is Social Media Different from Other Marketing?

Think of it like this: Social media is a digital version of every kind of print and physical advertising you have ever done. Where social media has the advantage, however, is that you can change up the message on a daily basis for a fraction of the cost. If you've been running your law firm for years, you've likely bought ad space in a newspaper, phone book, or even a billboard. These advertisements cost thousands of dollars for a static advertisement that is seen only by the people who subscribe to that publication or drive along that particular road where the billboard is located.

Social media, on the other hand, can transmit a different message every day to a custom audience based on the demographics of your ideal client. If you're a business attorney, you can target people who have interests in business and entrepreneurship, and even narrow it down to people whose job titles include things like "Founder," "Owner," etc. Whereas a billboard along the interstate could cost you up to five figures for a month and reach an unknown number of qualified people, a finely tuned social media audience can target thousands of people in your market.

It all starts with defining your objectives. What are you hoping for and expecting from your social media strategy? How will you measure success? If you don't take the time to think this through, you're flying blind.

Here's how we think most small law firms can best use social media:

1:To Build Top-of-Mind Awareness

Staying top-of-mind with your clients and your network is a critical part of maximizing your referrals. Social media provides an ideal channel to create quick touch-points multiple times per week.

2: To Enhance Credibility

Use social media as a platform to demonstrate your expertise and your status as a thought leader within your area of practice. Do this by sharing blog entries and articles you've written; posting news developments that impact your target market; and promoting media appearances, speaking opportunities, and other events that showcase your expertise.

3: To Build a Consistent Brand

Building an effective brand requires consistency and repetition. Use your social media presence to reinforce your focus and communicate it with your target market. Make it crystal clear *who* you work with and *what type* of work you do for them. Resist the temptation to post whatever crosses your mind that day and instead stay focused on building a consistent brand. (Your personal social media pages are for your regular, unfiltered thoughts.)

4: To Educate and Engage Your Audience

One of the most important functions of your internet foundation (of which social media is an integral part) is to condition and pre-educate potential clients and referral sources. It's an opportunity to set expectations for your clients. If done right, it can actually help you weed out clients who are not a good fit for your practice while at the same time attracting your ideal clients. We've had many clients tell us that their closing process is much faster, smoother, and more efficient as a result of their social media presence because the nightmare clients have been filtered out already and the good clients have been pre-educated and are excited to get the ball rolling.

Where Should Your Law Firm Post Content?

We recommend that all small law firms have a presence on the following social networks:

Facebook: There are over 1.62 BILLION active Facebook users, meaning they don't just have an account, they use the site at least once per day. Monthly visitors top out at over 2 billion. Simply put, every lawyer needs to have a presence there. Another key component to marketing on Facebook is that you can customize your audience and target your posts to reach a specific group of people—your target market.

Twitter: With over 500 million tweets posted daily, Twitter isn't too far behind Facebook when it comes to users and activity. Twitter is great because of all the engagement features—your followers can like, retweet, reply, move your tweets to a list, send messages, etc. The opportunities to network and have your content shared on Twitter are limitless, which is why we have found Twitter to be a powerful marketing tool.

LinkedIn: This platform is business-oriented and designed specifically for the working professional, which makes it an excellent place for connecting with potential clients and referral sources while building your network. One of the best features about LinkedIn is its networking capabilities. You can be rated and endorsed by your connections, which significantly boosts your credibility to anyone looking at your profile. Since LinkedIn is regarded as one of the more professional social media platforms, when someone does an internet search for you or your company, chances are they will check out your LinkedIn page if it pops up on the search results.

Action Item: Get on Social Media!

If you haven't done this yet, it's time to open up Facebook, Twitter, and LinkedIn and create profiles for your firm. If you're concerned about your own privacy and don't want to have your personal information associated with those profiles, don't worry! While you do need to connect a personal profile to Facebook and LinkedIn, no one sees your personal information. It's only connected on the back end to allow you access without having a separate login.

There are obviously differences from platform to platform, but the format for setting up your profile is basically the same—a photo or two and basic information about your firm. It's important to use the same photos across all platforms and that those photos match the branding of your website. You will have to crop them differently of course, but it's important to create brand consistency, and these visuals will help you accomplish that.

Instagram: Instagram is also extremely popular, especially among people aged 18-29. As an individual's age increases, the likelihood of being active on the app declines. But the popularity of this platform brings up the valid question: Should Instagram be used in a small law firm's marketing?

The short answer: Instagram can be a valuable part of your marketing strategy, but there are more important areas you should focus on first.

Instagram is an image-centric app for mobile phones. The only way to post images from a desktop is to manipulate the developer tools from your browser, which ultimately becomes more work than its worth. Also, because the app is centered so heavily on images, it's difficult to link back to your website because you can't embed hyperlinks in the images like you can on other platforms. You can include links on your profile page, but getting to that link requires an extra step for your followers, and a lot of times you'll lose people in the process even if it's as simple of an action as one click.

With that being said, Instagram can be helpful in maintaining your brand and coming across as personable and likable. A good use for Instagram with your law firm could be showcasing pictures of what happens behind the scenes, like members of your team in action. But remember, as important as the legal work you do is, a picture of you doing paperwork doesn't exactly make for a great photo.

If you have the fundamentals mentioned above in place working to cultivate your brand, then Instagram is a great option. Some additional ideas for images to post are quotes, events or outings your whole office participates in, video FAQ clips, and the occasional self-promotion. This could include a screenshot of a new feature on your website or a congratulatory post about a big case that you won. Of course, share that same post on your other social media channels so it gets even more exposure.

Avoid These Mistakes!

Unless you've been on social media since it became popular in the early 2000s, you might not be aware of some of the social etiquette that comes along with an active presence. Even if you're a social media veteran, the unspoken rules for businesses in how they present themselves to consumers is different from how you conduct yourself on your personal channels.

Here are some common mistakes that you should avoid making with your law firm's social media presence:

1: Creating a One-Way Conversation

Social media isn't meant to be used as if you're giving a speech to an audience. A better way to think of it is a cocktail party. It's an opportunity to interact with your audience, not just preach to them. Look for opportunities to generate engagement and interaction—don't just preach.

2: Constantly Trying to Make a Sale

Of course you want to grow your business, but bombarding your audience with a sales pitch over and over again won't work. You'll find yourself being ignored. Instead, look for opportunities to provide value to your audience. Share breaking news, industry tips, and helpful information such as blog entries or articles. Give your audience a reason to pay attention.

3: Creating Controversy

You should just avoid controversial subjects in general, regardless of how strongly you feel. There are exceptions to this depending on the nature of your business and your objectives, but at a minimum, if you're going to venture into controversial territory, make sure it is consistent with the brand you are seeking to create and make sure that it's not going to alienate your target audience. Remember that practically anything you post online could be seen by nearly anyone, so don't say anything on social media that you wouldn't say in front of a TV camera!

4: Losing Focus on Your Target Audience

Twitter, Facebook, and LinkedIn collectively have billions of members. That's a lot of people, and as a result it can be easy to lose focus. Remember who you're trying to engage (your target market) and don't shift your focus. For example, your law firm may be able to generate a bunch of likes and retweets by joking about the Grammy awards, but if that type of humor isn't consistent with your firm brand and doesn't appeal to your target market, it's going to do more harm than good.

5: Posting Inconsistently

Effective use of social media requires consistency. Posting feverishly for a day or two and then disappearing for three weeks won't allow relationships to develop and won't help you establish your brand. Even if it's just a post or two per week, make sure you're consistent.

6: Having Unrealistic Expectations

If you're expecting your social media presence to explode and result in tons of new business right off the bat, you're going to be disappointed. If you're looking for rapid returns, other forms of marketing are better suited for the task.

7: Lacking a Plan

If you don't have a plan, you're flying blind. What are you trying to accomplish? Who is your target market? How will you measure success? These questions (and more) are vital—you have to have a plan!

Create Your System

Well over 60 million businesses have Facebook pages. Millions more have a presence on Twitter and on LinkedIn. Yet many (probably the majority) of these pages and profiles sit dormant. The business owner or an employee took the time to create a presence and perhaps start using it but lost interest within a few weeks.

This happens all the time. Business owners hear about the power of social media, decide to dip their toes in the water, but eventually lose interest. Most of the time, they stop because the real world intervenes, they deal with some form of a crisis, and they forget about their fledgling social media presence.

Given that social media requires consistency over time in order to provide a return, this is a real problem. So here's our advice: If you're going to get involved with social media, don't do it without a plan and a system.

This process isn't complicated. First, identify the various platforms you want to use. Simple enough, right? Step two is determining how frequently you're going to publish to each of them. There's no right or wrong answer, although we recommend posting several times a week.

Once you've determined how frequently you want to publish to various platforms, it's just a matter of creating a schedule to ensure that it happens. We recommend scheduling these tasks into your week, just like anything else on your to-do list. Remember to take these tasks seriously—you wouldn't just skip a meeting with an important client, and you shouldn't skip your social media efforts either.

If this sounds overwhelming, don't worry. You have options. One option is delegating, either to an employee, family member, or an outside agency. (If you do decide to delegate, it's important that you follow up and make sure that the system is being executed.) Another option is using programs to help you schedule this activity in advance. For instance, you could spend a Saturday composing your social media posts for the entire month. Then, using a program like Hootsuite, you can schedule the content to be published throughout the month. This way, you've taken care of a month's worth of social media in one sitting.

Finally, if you're concerned about committing time and resources, remember that it doesn't have to happen all at once. If you'd prefer to start with just a single platform, by all means do so. You can always grow your presence as you become more comfortable.

At the end of the day, social media marketing requires a commitment. If you're not willing to make it, wait until you're ready to get involved. When you ARE ready to begin growing your business through social media, remember that it starts with a plan and a system. Otherwise, you're just spinning your wheels.

Engage with Your Audience

While you've heard that you have to be on social media, the fact is that social media platforms like Facebook, Twitter, and LinkedIn offer the opportunity to reach a virtually unlimited audience for little to no cost. But there is more to building an effective presence than simply creating a profile and waiting for the business to roll in. You need to actually participate in the social media community and engage with your audience.

Here are a few ways you can do that:

1: Share Pictures

One of the primary goals of most businesses on Facebook is to go viral. The concept is simple—as users comment, like, and share your posts, their friends are exposed to your content. For that reason, posting content that generates a response from your audience, even if it's as simple as a like, is key. Studies have conclusively shown that posting images is the best way to do this—likely because it's very easy for the audience to engage. Whether it's a picture of your team on the job, an interesting infographic, or even a comic strip to brighten your audience's day, sharing images must be a part of your regular strategy.

2: Ask Questions

Facebook allows you to poll your audience—and it's very easy both to create and to participate in. Everyone wants to feel that their opinion matters, and your Facebook audience is no exception. Ask them what they'd like you to cover in your next blog series. Ask them which team they are pulling for in the big game tonight. Remember, it doesn't have to be all business, all the time—the goal is to build relationships Just make sure what you post is consistent with your brand!

3: Update Your Audience When News Breaks

When events that will impact your market occur, share them! As a tax attorney, for instance, keep your audience up to date on recent laws that relate to the tax code and explain the potential impact.

4: Share Valuable Information

Provide value to your audience. Sharing news, as discussed above, is one way to do this. You can also share blog posts, helpful tips, and other information. At the end of the day, if you aren't providing value to your audience, they're going to tune you out.

5: Host a Contest

Consider hosting a contest in which your audience can win a prize. Maybe you hold a raffle in which entrants are anyone who signs up for your newsletter during a certain period. Maybe the prize goes to anyone who has followed or liked your page during a certain period. You have a lot of options.

The Facebook Focus

Facebook marketing is absolutely a game changer for business, and yet many internet marketers make Facebook out to be a magic pill or a perfect, complete marketing solution for every single business, product, or campaign. If this is what you're expecting from Facebook, you're going to be disappointed. In other words, Facebook is great, but it shouldn't be your sole marketing avenue.

What can a Facebook presence really accomplish for your business? Here are a few things:

1: Create Measurable Brand Exposure

Your Facebook presence allows you to regularly post content for your audience to see. This content can be in the form of a text-only post, an image, a video, or a link, to name a few. This gives you the opportunity to build your brand and connect with your audience. The best part is that it's all trackable.

Within hours of creating a post, you can know exactly how many people have seen it, how many of them have clicked on it, and how many have shared it with their Facebook friends. This gives you the ability to figure out exactly what's working and what's not so you can fine tune your strategy to ensure that your content is resonating with your audience.

2: Drive Traffic to Your Website or Blog

By posting content on your Facebook business page, you have the opportunity to drive traffic anywhere, including to your own site. Whether it is posting a link to a recent blog entry, a special offer, or a particular landing page, you can direct your audience wherever you'd like them to go. Be careful, however. If all you're doing is spamming your audience with self-promoting posts, they're going to learn to ignore you. The key is to provide value by posting helpful or entertaining information, and sprinkling in promotional posts along the way.

3: Generate a New Point of Contact with Customers and Prospects

It's important to maintain top-of-mind awareness with your customers, but this can be a challenge if you typically go long periods of time without seeing your customers or clients. An accountant, for instance, may only speak to his clients a few times each year. Connecting on Facebook allows you to continue to strengthen your relationship and your brand positioning, even with customers you haven't seen face-to-face in months.

4: Provides Potential for Viral Marketing

The interconnected nature of Facebook offers the ability not only to reach your immediate audience, but also their circle of friends, and their circle's circle of friends, and so on. This is because when a fan of your business likes your content or shares it, their friends will see this activity. If it's compelling content, they may well decide to share it with their friends, and so forth.

This phenomenon explains how seemingly random pictures or videos can reach an audience in the millions. Now, it's unlikely that your content will achieve exposure on this scale, but the same concept allows you to gradually increase your audience and reach more potential customers. If you're providing valuable content, the word will spread.

Chapter 10 ~ Break Down Barriers with Video

If you don't have video on your law firm website, you are missing a huge opportunity. Here are three reasons why your site absolutely, positively, no-doubt-about-it needs to include video:

1: Video Establishes a Personal Connection

One of the key challenges that lawyers face is *establishing trust* in potential clients. These potential clients are facing a significant life or business challenge and they are likely going to commit a large sum of money to address it. They aren't going to make this decision lightly, and they certainly aren't going to hire a lawyer that they don't trust.

Short of a face-to-face conversation, video is the best medium for building a personal connection and inspiring trust. Whether you present yourself this way or not, people are typically intimidated by lawyers. Video gives your them the opportunity to hear your voice, see your face, and get a feel for your body language and the way you carry yourself, which allows them to feel more comfortable around you.

2: Video Establishes Credibility and Professionalism

Well-produced video makes you look credible. Crisp footage and quality audio sends a powerful message about your professionalism and your dedication to your craft. It's an opportunity to separate yourself from other lawyers who aren't willing to invest the time and resources to create quality video.

3: Many Web Visitors Would Rather Watch Video Than Read Text

A number of surveys in recent years have confirmed that many website users would rather watch a video than read text. Not only that, but they are more likely to share a video with their network than they are to share text. Video is perfect for use on social media as well. Video shouldn't *replace* text on your website, but you should use it to complement written content and other resources.

This list could go on indefinitely because there are numerous benefits to including video on your website with very few downsides.

What Do You Shoot?

Hopefully at this point you know that you should do some type of video as part of your marketing efforts. After all, video increases a consumer's understanding of your product or service by 74%. Not to mention, many are more likely to watch a video than read through content.

So what exactly should you do for video and how do you use it? We have some a few ideas:

1: Create a Video Series

There are a few directions you can go with a video series, but we prefer FAQs. Think of the most common questions your prospects have. This can be about your services, but more importantly, it should be the questions and concerns they have about the legal issue they are facing. The best part of a series like this is that it needs no script! Hire a videographer, create a list of good questions, and give your natural 30-60 second answer for each. Now you have a FAQ video series you can leverage in your internet marketing efforts.

2: Video Introduction

Create a short video, maybe a minute or so, where you introduce yourself and what you do. This is likely best on the homepage of your website. An introduction video is an opportunity to do just that—introduce yourself to your prospects. Give them a chance to see you and hear you in order to break down those barriers we mentioned above. Additionally, it's an opportunity to share more about what you do and how you might be able to help with their situation. The idea behind this type of video is that it helps a prospect feel more comfortable about calling you or scheduling a consultation.

3: Explain Your Services

Similar to the FAQ series, this would be a set of videos explaining your different services. For example, let's say you are a real estate attorney and you have a pages on your website for titles, foreclosure, and short sales. You could create a short video for each page where you share a bit more about what you do in each practice area.

There is certainly more you can do with video, but sometimes the most simple ideas are the most effective. Be casual, be yourself, and share good information. You don't need to create a commercial!

How to Present Yourself

One of the biggest objections we hear from lawyers as to why they don't want to do video is the concern over how they look on video. However, we have never had any of our clients trolled for how they look in their videos, mainly because the people watching them aren't concerned about appearance. People are watching your videos to get information, not to be entertained or to kill time.

Body image issues are a real problem and even though we're not psychologists, we can tell you that how you appear on your videos is the least of your viewers' concerns. Of course, you don't want to make a complete fool of yourself, especially if you're not used to being on camera. That's why we always remind our video clients of these specific points before a video shoot:

1: Be Yourself

Act as though you are having a conversation with the person behind the camera. That will make your viewers feel as if the natural next step is to come in to your office, sit down, and continue the conversation with you.

2: Use High Quality Audio

Obviously your video needs to be high quality. These days, it's not hard to shoot a video that looks great. But just as importantly, and much harder to get right, is the quality of your audio. Poor audio quality makes your video seem cheap and unprofessional. It's worth investing in good equipment or hiring a professional videographer to make sure you get the audio right.

3: Look at the Camera

It's very noticeable when you look away from the camera or shift your eyes, even just a little bit. It can make you appear nervous or even untrustworthy. You also don't need to be artsy and creative and have a camera angle that makes it look like you're being interviewed. Simply look at the camera for the duration of the video.

4: Don't Fidget or Pace

Be expressive! Use your hands if that's how you communicate, but don't fidget and don't move back and forth. These movements may feel natural at the time, but on camera they are distracting and can look odd. Hold your position relative to the camera.

5: Think Carefully About Your Positioning

For some people, standing to shoot video is much more natural. For others, sitting is more comfortable. There is no universal right or wrong answer, but what's important is that you figure out which position is more natural for you and choose accordingly.

6: Choose Relevant Topics

Are there questions that you get over and over in consultations? Are there certain misconceptions that you find yourself addressing repeatedly with your clients? Chances are, these would make a great topic for a video. The idea is to create videos addressing these common questions so that prospective clients come to see you as a trusted resource who understands what they are going through and is in a position to help.

7: Keep Your Videos Short

Try to keep your answers between 30-60 seconds. You don't need to give a technical breakdown of each question—instead, provide an overview and explain any practical implications. The average visitor to your website simply doesn't have the patience to watch a 10 minute video.

8: Don't Script Your Answers

The most effective videos present you as comfortable, relaxed, and in command. When you script your videos, you're likely to come off as robotic. Your FAQs cover topics that you discuss regularly in your law practice, so there's no need to script! You know this stuff like the back of your hand, so have confidence in your ability to communicate.

Of course we're not saying you can't prepare at all. It's a good practice to have a loose idea of what you're going to cover in each response. Take a few seconds before each video to gather your thoughts, but don't overthink it and don't script your response. You want your videos to feel conversational, not robotic.

Using Your Videos in Your Marketing

Like we've mentioned already, video is a huge opportunity to enhance your marketing. However, simply having a stash of videos is pointless if you're not using them as part of your marketing efforts. Here are a few ways you can integrate your videos:

1: Upload Them to YouTube

You can't do anything with your videos if they're stuck on your phone or computer. They need to live somewhere online. While there are other options out there such as Vimeo, YouTube is your best bet. When uploading them, be sure to include a description, a link to your website, and use relevant tags.

2: Use Them on Your Website

This might be the most obvious answer, but let's dig a bit deeper into it. How you use your video on your website matters. First, embed them from YouTube rather than uploading it directly to your site because the large video file will likely slow down your website's loading speed.

Additionally, don't just stick your video anywhere. If its an introduction video, put it front and center on your home page. If you have a video series such as FAQs, create a video library section on your website or release them as a series, such as posting one each month. Like a continuously updated blog, a video library that gets updated on a regular basis gives visitors a reason to keep coming back.

3: Share Them on Social Media

Video, like photos, has better engagement than text, so social media is a great place to share your videos. If you added your videos to your website, and not just YouTube, you should be able to link to the video on your website. It's much better to send someone to your website than YouTube, right?

If you've gotten really comfortable with social media, you can also upload your videos natively to Facebook so they play automatically as someone scrolls past on your timeline. There is also software out there that automatically transcribes your videos for you, which acts as an extra attention-grabber as someone scrolls through their timeline.

4: Add It to Your E-Newsletter

Video is a great opportunity to make your e-newsletter stand out from the rest. Not only will it look more visually engaging, but for those who don't like to read very much, perhaps they will click play! Again, if the video is on your website, then they will click play within the e-newsletter, which will take them to your website to watch it!

The bottom line: Video enhances what you're doing online. It breaks down the barriers and fears people have of you, it makes your website more impressive, and it makes your social media and e-newsletters more interesting. Most importantly, well done video creates credibility, making your look like the expert!

Chapter 11 ~ Understand Your Marketing Data

It's one thing to have a robust online marketing campaign, but how can you tell if it's actually successful if you don't track any data? A lot of lawyers install Google Analytics on their website (which, by the way, if you don't have Google Analytics installed, stop reading right now and get that taken care of because it's really important) and then don't bother to look at the numbers. Even worse, they look at the wrong numbers because they were never told what was really important.

It is vitally important that you consistently review your marketing data. If you're not taking a look at least once per month, there is no way that your internet presence is as effective as it could be. These statistics tell you much more than simply how many visitors your website is receiving or how many people have visited your most recent blog. It tells you what's working and what's not.

One of the biggest problems lawyers face in the marketing world is that marketing companies like to throw a lot of data at you and then gloat at how their work has resulted in an increase in various metrics. Unfortunately for you, a lot of that data is useless. Those numbers are mostly for vanity and don't really give you any insight into how well your marketing is doing.

It's understandable. After all, it's easier for a marketing company to try to get you to focus on data that isn't making you money as long as those numbers are contorted to make themselves look good. This might hurt your feelings, but the following data points you've likely been tracking for years aren't really contributing to your overall success:

1: Open Rate

When it comes to your emails, an open rate doesn't pain the entire picture. Open rates only account for—obviously—people who open your email. It doesn't tell you who saw your email enter their inbox and then for whatever reason ignored it. However, the fact that they still saw your email has value because they were still reminded you existed.

2: Bounce Rate

Of course you want people to navigate to multiple pages of your website in a single session, but if you're consistently posting blogs, videos, and other educational information on social media and through various other channels, the chances of you having a higher bounce rate is pretty high. And that's okay! People need to have several interactions with you before they are moved to take action, so multiple visits to your website where someone views a single page isn't necessarily a bad thing.

3: Website Visitors

You should be wary of any marketing company that tells you they will increase your web traffic. If you see your visitor numbers climb and climb without ever plateauing, something fishy is going on. Regardless of your market size, your website will only attract so many visitors. Marketing companies have been guilty of sending irrelevant traffic to sites through nefarious tactics just to boost traffic numbers.

So what data should you be tracking? It's simple—whatever numbers that provide a direct result from your marketing efforts. Whatever you're paying your marketing company to do is what you should be tracking. If a company promises 100 leads each month, that's what you should track.

Because we are helping our clients increase their referrals and attract better clients, there are two primary metrics that we ask clients to monitor:

1. **Referrals**: We expect our clients to see an increase in referrals. Obviously we don't believe those referrals will continue to increase. They will certainly plateau at some point, but they should remain consistent at a higher level than before.

2. **Average Case Value**: When you put a premium brand in place and implement a consistent marketing strategy, you begin to attract the right kinds of clients and do the type of work you really want to

do. This allows you to command higher rates. That means your average case value should increase over time.

But even if you implement a different marketing strategy, there are certain other metrics you should pay attention to, including:

1: Traffic Sources
How are visitors finding their way to your website? How effective are your social media platforms in terms of generating traffic? This information is critical when it comes to evaluating the effectiveness of your internet marketing presence.

2: Landing Pages
Where are visitors entering your website? Are they starting at your home page, or are they following links that may lead them to your contact page or your blog? Many website visitors won't view more than a single page, so it's important that your landing pages are effective. If visitors are frequently landing on pages that are less compelling, figure out a way to direct them to more effective pages instead.

3: Exit Pages
Where are visitors leaving your website? If a specific page is generating more than its fair share of exits, there may be a problem. This data is particularly important because it allows you to evaluate your sales funnel and identify areas of weakness.

4: Visitor Location
Where, geographically, are your visitors located? If you're a local business in Tampa, visitors from California aren't going to be worth much. If you're generating traffic from locations outside of your target market, you are wasting resources—but you won't know it if you don't evaluate the data.

As an attorney, you have a lot to keep track of, but your marketing data should be one of the most important items on your list. At the end of the day, if you continue to be frustrated with your marketing and you can't pinpoint the reason why, you only have yourself to blame. It's easy to blame a marketing company and go somewhere else (why do you think there are so many options out there?), but as a business owner, you should be fully aware of the data that's available to you and hold your marketing company (or your in-house marketing person) accountable for delivering on what they promised.

<u>Action Item:</u> Understand Your Data

If you're doing your marketing yourself, go find your data and really look to see if it's performing well. If you have a marketing company or an in-house staff member doing it, have them explain the numbers to you and have them tell you exactly what their goals are.

If you find that these conversations aren't providing you with solid answers that you understand 100%, it's time to either light a fire under their chairs or cut ties and start over. But don't make this a one-time task. Make it a recurring weekly or monthly task to check in on your marketing data to make sure you are happy with the results.

Chapter 12 ~ SEO (And Why It Sucks)

No internet marketing book these days is complete without something on Search Engine Optimization. However, we at Spotlight Branding take a different approach to SEO.

Despite all of the great information and crystal clear roadmaps that are contained in this book, lawyers still believe that SEO is their only and best option. It's not true, and we would be remiss if we didn't explain why.

Action Item: Google a Lawyer

Go to Google and type in a search for a particular type of attorney in your city. For example, search "business lawyer Phoenix" or "bankruptcy attorney Boston." Here is what you'll see:

1. You will first see three results with a green "Ad" box next to the URL. These come from Google Ads via their AdWords program, otherwise known as pay-per-click ads.

2. Next you will see a map showing you all of the attorneys in that particular practice area in that particular city. Some show up from Google Ads, some show up because of SEO.

3. Below the map you have 10 listings and three more ad results. Those 10 listings are important because 4-6 of those listings are for directories and review sites like Yelp.

Keep that search result in mind and reference it as you read the rest of this chapter.

On a broader level, SEO is an attempt by engineers and coders to manipulate Google's algorithms in order to rank higher on any given search phrase. That involves a lot of work considering Google changes its algorithms as many as 600 times every year. Even more, talking to an SEO "expert" is a fruitless endeavor because you never truly get an explanation as to what actually goes on behind the scenes to make it work for you.

Because you as an attorney are not (likely) a tech geek, SEO companies have spent years taking advantage of your lack of knowledge of how the internet works, which ends up costing you thousands of dollars and months of frustration. Here's a brief—and hopefully somewhat simple—explanation of several elements that go into SEO work:

1: Keyword Density

As Google and other search engine technologies become more advanced, it has developed the ability to *mimic* what an actual human does when searching for information. A website that regularly produces content, such as blogs, video, etc., is going to catch Google's eye more often than a stagnant website. Even more, "evergreen content," or content that holds relevance over a long period of time, holds much more value and has a higher potential to appear in search results. However, the majority of SEO companies offer a large quantity of blog articles stuffed with keywords to attract Google's crawler bots and rush that site up the rankings.

Because those articles are written for bots rather than the people who are reading them, it creates a poor user experience (UX). Beyond just a higher quantity of articles, there are competing theories about how many keywords need to be within the headlines, the first 100 words, and in the article overall. It turns marketing and copywriting into a science rather than a human connection.

2: Site Speed

Google takes site load times into consideration as part of its algorithm in determining where a site ranks in search results. Ways to improve site load times include embedding media files from YouTube rather than loading a massive file directly onto the site, as well as compressing images and other files so that they take up as little space as possible.

What SEO companies like to do, however, is send you a "report" of a "test" they ran that shows you how slow your site is. The problem is that those speed tests are blown out of proportion because SEO companies know you aren't smart enough to know what they mean. Those tests are color coded for simplicity, and we as humans are programmed to see that RED = BAD and freak out. In turn, you get mad at your webmaster, cancel your contract, and have your website and marketing switched to a new company, where the cycle starts all over again.

Here's the thing: The overwhelming majority (if not all) of those tests come from Google PageSpeed. However, even though it's coming from Google, it actually has nothing to do with SEO. Even more, those speed tests are giving your website a poor score for embedded codes and third party sites connected to your website, such as Facebook, Google Analytics, YouTube, and other sources your site might pull from for any reason. You can't control those sites' speeds, but those tests penalize you if they're loading slowly.

The only metric that truly matters from those tests is TTFB (Time to First Byte). In other words, it's the amount of time it takes your browser to load the very first tiny byte from your site. The problem there—and this is where it gets complicated—is that a slow TTFB could also be a server issue (i.e, where your website is hosted) or a network issue (i.e, there are too many people on your WiFi and it's slowing the overall speed down) rather than your website actually being the problem.

<u>Action Item:</u> Do a PageSpeed Test

Go to Google and search for "PageSpeed Insights." From there, run a check on a bigger company's website to see what their test results show. Guess what you'll find? Everyone fails the test in some way, whether it's desktop load time, mobile load time, etc. While speed does matter from a UX standpoint, it doesn't completely destroy an SEO score.

In fact—and this is going to blow your mind—Google doesn't even care about its own PageSpeed suggestions for its own properties (do a test of YouTube and you'll see what we mean). So the next time an SEO company sends you the results of a test that was run on your site, just consider it spam.

3: Internal Linking

A website that links to itself internally has several SEO benefits. First, internal linking (where appropriate) allows visitors to follow a track for more info. Second, it improves search results for certain keywords. Third, it allows Google to more easily crawl and index the site. Just don't flood each page with a ton of other links to other areas of your site—do it where it's appropriate.

4: Link Sharing / Back Linking

The concept of link sharing deals with putting a website's URL inside the content of another website, and vice versa. This is an old SEO tactic that Google is starting to move away from because it can easily be taken advantage of. For example, an SEO company, in an attempt to drive traffic and increase rankings in keyword searches, can paste a URL on websites in different markets and businesses.

This means your website could begin to appear in irrelevant searches (i.e, if you're an attorney in Georgia, you could appear in searches for an Arizona attorney). From an ethical standpoint, you could become associated with other attorneys or businesses that you may not endorse.

103

5: Meta Descriptions, Schema, and Tags

This is an older SEO trick that's becoming less and less relevant when it comes to your ranking (they're pretty important for UX, though). Meta descriptions act as the first few lines of teaser text underneath a search result on a Google search. The schema works along these lines as well and is a way to basically customize how you want each page's title to appear in a Google ranking search.

Tags are pieces of code that are programmed into the site. These pieces of code tell Google what a particular portion of the website is. There are two primary sections, <head> and <body>. From there, different elements of the page are entered into the markup.

6: Image Tags

If you want your website to appear in an image search, you add alt-tags to the media on your site. Because Google can't technically see images, adding alt-tags to images lets Google know what that image is and if it's relevant to a search.

7: Hidden Text

An easy way to stuff keywords and make a page more attractive for SEO purposes is to insert a block of text full of geographic locations and common keywords into the code of the site. It won't appear on the live site because it lacks any sort of visual directive. However, when Google crawls the site, it will still see it. Like link sharing, this is an SEO practice that Google is placing less importance on.

Is your head spinning yet? If you still aren't entirely sure what actually goes into SEO work, you're not alone. So why do so many attorneys blindly throw money at it and hope for the best?

SEO isn't a necessary part of your law firm marketing strategy. You can win clients without even worrying about your ranking on Google. In fact, focusing too much of your marketing strategy on SEO can actually hurt your firm and slow your growth.

There's a narrative, which is unfortunately widely accepted, that you have no choice but to spend money on SEO if you want to grow your law firm. That it's automatic, that it's required, and that you'd be crazy not to spend money on search engine optimization.

Have you ever noticed that it's the SEO providers themselves who are pushing this message? That the very people who profit from selling SEO are the ones telling you that it's non-negotiable? SEO is a marketing **option**. That's it. An option. It's one way, among many, many ways, for you to get new clients and grow your law firm.

It's not the only way.

It's not required.

It's not the best way!

Consider this scenario: Let's say you've created a physical flyer promoting your law firm. It's a very nice flyer and you want a lot of people to see it. How are you going to make sure that people see it? You have a lot of options!

You could send someone down to a street-corner to pass out the flyers. You could mail them out. You could put them on windshields. You could put stacks of them in local coffee shops.

What's the best approach? That depends on many other factors like your marketing budget, the type of client you want to attract, what your competitors are doing, and more. The point is, you have options, and you get to make the decision.

In this analogy, the flyer represents your website. You've got a website, it looks nice, and you want people to visit it. You could choose the SEO route, just like you could choose to send someone walking through the street handing out flyers. Imagine then, when you sent someone out on the street to pass out your flyers, you found out that the street was packed with a hundred other people passing out flyers too. Pretty quickly, you'd look for another strategy, right? That's what's happening on Google.

If you do a search for "Family Lawyers in Charlotte NC," you'll get 3,550,000 results. There aren't actually 3.5 million lawyers in Charlotte, but there are 3.5 million web pages competing for that search phrase.

For reference, there are 7.8 million results for criminal law attorneys in Minneapolis, 15.5 million results for bankruptcy attorneys in Los Angeles, and 59.3 million results for business lawyers in Miami! Even a smaller town like Topeka, Kansas, returns 268,000 results when you search for "Immigration Lawyer" and there are only 126,000 people in Topeka!

Here's the problem: SEO is a zero-sum game. There is only one position at the top of Google for any one search term. That means if you want to take over that top spot, the only way you can do so is by taking it away from someone else. Just think about how many lawyers do what you do in your city. There may be hundreds, but even if it's only a few dozen, you're all competing for the same space on Google, and only one person can win the race.

Why would you spend thousands of dollars on something that most likely won't even work out for you? Would you pay $1,000 per month for the *possibility* of appearing on a billboard if you knew that hundreds of other lawyers were also paying for that same possibility, but only one of you could win? Of course not! But that's exactly what happens when you join the rat race for Google rankings. The only people that are really winning in this scenario are the SEO companies that are cashing your checks each month.

And maybe you don't really care about being the *first* result on a search. However, if you return to our *Action Item* at the beginning of this chapter, you only really have the opportunity to take one of 4-6 spots on the front page. The other half are controlled by directories and review sites. What's most disheartening of all is that the lawyers who actually made it to the first page are usually the mega firms in your city with a marketing budget that dwarfs yours. They're spending five figures each month just on SEO, not to mention other marketing efforts. Our guess is that, as a solo attorney, you do not have anything resembling that much of a marketing budget.

That's why we preach our strategy. While your competitors are blowing their marketing budgets on SEO, you can use that money to maximize your referrals and create a chain of happy clients and repeat business rather than one-off customers who only care about how low your rates are. While you're creating a premium brand and user experience with your digital marketing, your competitors are trying to appease Google bots in hopes of showing up on the first page of a particular search result.

Chapter 13 ~ Working with the Right Marketing Company

Surely you didn't receive a book written by a marketing company and not expect something about hiring a marketing company, right? We promise this won't be a sales pitch to enroll in our services.

As a solo attorney, your time is too valuable to be bogged down by all of the work that goes into marketing your firm, especially when you're also doing a lot of the backend tasks that come with running a business *and* actually doing the legal work. While we can't speak to how you run the rest of your business, there's a reason there are so many legal marketing companies out there competing for your attention—it just makes sense to offload that work and delegate it to someone else.

Even if you choose to work with someone other than Spotlight Branding, we want to make sure you consider every angle. Choosing the right marketing company can be a headache. There's certainly no shortage of options, and it's often hard to know what to believe!

We've heard some amazing marketing horror stories over the years. Money wasted and promises unfulfilled are a common narrative in the legal marketing world. That said, the right marketing is key to creating a thriving practice, especially one that helps you achieve your goals and create predictable (and growing) revenue.

Our hope is that this chapter helps you weed through the B.S. by providing you with three essential tips for choosing the right marketing company for your law firm:

1: Make Sure There Is Strategic Alignment

The next time you speak to a marketing provider, ask them **why** they do the things they do. Overall, you want to know what they believe about marketing. What's their strategy and philosophy? You may find that many marketing providers have a rather vague answer.

You would expect a marketing company to be very strategic. However, most rarely discuss their strategy and what they believe about marketing. Instead, they want to focus on showing you examples (e.g. how pretty everything looks) and numbers of how some of their (best) clients are performing as a way to pressure you into signing up!

As for Spotlight Branding, we have a very specific approach to building websites, writing content, and getting results. We're intentional about the things we do and speak a great deal about our strategy with prospective clients. What we believe has to be a good fit with your firm's vision so we know if there's alignment.

Before you begin your search, make sure you have clarity and direction on what you want. At that point, it will become much easier to check for strategic alignment with the potential marketing partners you're considering. Keep in mind that some marketing companies focus more on volume of clients while others focus on getting you better quality clients. Some may focus on branding and referrals, while others rely on search engines.

2: Consider Different Forms of ROI

At the end of the day, marketing comes down to ROI (return on investment). It's important that both you and your marketing provider are clear on what the expected ROI will be. We can't stress enough how important it is to have that conversation.

Remember, however, that ROI can take different forms. In some cases, it's as simple as money spent on advertising that equated to new leads. But not every lawyer just wants more clients. Some lawyers want better quality clients. "Better" might mean higher paying, or it might mean more clients in a specific practice area.

Spotlight Branding focuses strongly on branding and referrals. Our ROI usually comes in the form of increased referrals, better quality clients, and an improved ROI from all other business development efforts. At the end of the day, you need to do what we suggested earlier and track your data. That's the only way you'll be able to measure the true ROI of your marketing.

Lastly, don't just assume that ROI is as simple as "*I need more clients.*" Consider what you really want and how the right marketing can help you get there.

3: Be Logical

It's really easy to get caught up in the excitement of a good sales presentation or in the promise of a great salesperson. With marketing, it's easy to get shiny object syndrome. If you find yourself in this situation, simply take a step back and consider what you're being offered. Does it sound right, or is it too good to be true? Is what you are being promised what you really need?

For example, logic tends to fall short when discussing SEO. It's hard to have a conversation these days about a website without SEO being part of the plan. But as we discussed in the previous chapter, it's a highly competitive landscape with limited real estate when it comes to people searching for a specific legal service.

In the end, not every lawyer will have success with SEO. In fact, not every lawyer needs SEO or needs to be at the top of Google's search ranking to be a successful law practice.

So when it comes to logic, think about this: How is it that nearly every marketing company out there can sell SEO with limited space? How can that really work in the long run? It's the equivalent of 100 lawyers competing for the same roadside billboard and hiring the same company to do so. If you slow down and think about it, it doesn't add up!

We hope you found all of the information and advice in this book helpful. Whether we opened your eyes to a new way of thinking about your marketing or we reaffirmed what you already believed, we hope that you're now thinking about the right strategy for your firm. The decisions you make moving forward could mean finding the growth you've been looking for, or you could continue the same cycle of frustration you've been experiencing since you've been marketing your firm. Which way will you go?

<u>Action Item:</u> Talk to Us!

If you have any questions about the strategies or talking points we've written about in this book, give us a call at 800-406-7229 or send us an email at info@spotlightbranding.com. We will be happy to talk to you about your marketing strategy.

Bonus Tips

We hope you got a lot of information and inspiration from this book. As you move forward and implement the strategies in this book, we wanted to leave you with 10 last bonus tips for how you can kick your marketing and the brand you've created up a notch.

Remember, your marketing strategy is the key to growing your law firm. If your marketing strategy is stale (or non-existent) you're not going to fuel the growth you're hoping for. On the other hand, an effective marketing strategy will help you bring in new clients, generate more referrals, and even help you justify higher rates.

Here are ten final ideas to get your wheels turning. Don't try to implement all of these at once. We recommend focusing on just one or two initiatives at a time and then adding more as you develop a rhythm.

1: Launch a Podcast

Podcasting has exploded as a media source—25% of Americans listen to podcasts every week. Launching a podcast geared towards your target market is an effective strategy that you can use to educate potential clients, keep them engaged, and build your credibility at the same time.

Plus, it's easier than you think. We have a podcast at Spotlight Branding call The Law Firm Marketing Minute. We simply record an episode (all you need is a voice recording app on your phone!), upload it to a host who distributes it to Apple Podcasts and other apps, and then share it across our social channels and website. It doesn't take a tech nerd to accomplish!

Best of all, if you already have a healthy blog and video library, you already have your content for your podcast! Since a podcast is audio-based, you've now completely encompassed the primary ways we consume information—reading, watching, and listening. Your episodes don't have to be hours long like some shows (our podcast episodes are almost always under 10 minutes). Rather, just take as long as you need in order to address your topic of the week.

2: Host Events

Creating and hosting in-person events for potential clients and referral sources can generate momentum and enthusiasm for your practice. We've seen clients take this strategy in many different directions, from hosting monthly informational sessions, to holding quarterly VIP parties, to organizing seminars featuring expert speakers on topics of interest to business owners.

3: Sharpen Your Referral Strategy

Referrals are a primary source of new business for most law firms, and clients who are referred to you are typically among the most pleasant and profitable to work with. Start by identifying your top referral sources and invest time and energy into deepening those relationships. Identify other individuals who are strategically positioned to send a high volume of work your way and create relationships with them as well. Consider creating referral incentives or even holding regular referral competitions to keep your entire network engaged.

4: Target Appropriate Sponsorships

Sponsorships can be a big waste of money if you take the wrong approach. Do NOT jump on every opportunity that comes your way. We've seen firms spend large sums of money sponsoring organizations, events, or publications that have little-to-no relevance to their target market. On the other hand, if you can identify groups, events, websites, or magazines that your clients are engaged with, sponsorship can make a great deal of sense.

5: Offer Additional Value to Current and Past Clients

Oftentimes there is more work to be done for your past and even current clients. They just don't know they need it yet or they don't know that you can provide the solution. Solve both problems by creating an audit or evaluation for your clients. The goal is simple: Ask them questions about their business, their estate plan, their family life, whatever it may be, and look for ways you can continue to help with their legal issues.

6: Publish a Book

There's arguably no greater tool to establish your credibility and your expertise in your area of practice than publishing a book. While it might sound overwhelming, you can easily use the blogs that you've written over time and repurpose them into a book. If you have a marketing person on your team, assign them to organize this content into an outline. Then, create new content as needed to fill holes and create cohesion.

7: Network Smarter

Networking is a valuable strategy for drumming up referrals and new business, particularly if you're in the "more time than money" phase of your firm. But it's important to manage your investment well. Don't simply attend every event in your area. Instead, identify a small handful of targeted organizations that have great potential and get heavily involved.

8: Speak

Speaking positions you as an expert and an authority. It's a great way to attract new clients, too. Look for opportunities to educate your audience while building your expertise at the same time. This can include presentations on changing laws and regulations that impact your industry, tips and strategies for your market, best practices for avoiding legal disputes, and more.

9: Launch a Joint Venture

Who can you join forces with to provide a uniquely valuable product or service for your clients? The advantages to this approach are significant. It represents an opportunity to earn additional income from your existing clients; but more importantly, it also gives you access to your partner's clients and customers in the venture.

10: Train Your Staff to Recognize and Capitalize on Opportunities

Your staff likely knows people that could use your services or will encounter them in their daily life, and they've seen firsthand how your firm creates value for your clients. Teach them how to recognize potential clients, how to engage them, and how to connect them with you (or whoever handles the intake process for your firm). This doesn't have to be a complicated process and it frankly shouldn't be hard for your team to execute.

We've covered a lot of ground here, and hopefully you've gleaned a few ideas that could work for your firm. But it's important to be realistic about this—don't bite off more than you can chew. We suggest that you identify one (or two at most) new initiatives to start with. When you find something that works well, make it a part of your ongoing marketing system and then move on to the next new idea.